Merchandising Made Simple

Merchandising Made Simple

Using Standards and Dynamite Displays to Boost Circulation

Jenny LaPerriere and Trish Christiansen

LIBRARIES

U N L I M I T E D

A Member of the Greenwood Publishing Group

Westport, Connecticut • London

Library of Congress Cataloging-in-Publication Data

LaPerriere, Jenny, 1970–
    Merchandising made simple : using standards and dynamite displays
    to boost circulation / Jenny LaPerriere and Trish Christiansen.
        p. cm.
    Includes bibliographical references and index.
    ISBN 978-1-59158-561-9 (alk. paper)
    1. Library exhibits. I. Christiansen, Trish, 1971– II. Title.
    Z717.L37   2008
    021.7—dc22   2008003687

British Library Cataloguing in Publication Data is available.

Library of Congress Catalog Card Number: 2008003687
ISBN: 978-1-59158-561-9

First published in 2008

Libraries Unlimited, 88 Post Road West, Westport, CT 06881
A Member of the Greenwood Publishing Group, Inc.
www.lu.com

Printed in the United States of America

The paper used in this book complies with the
Permanent Paper Standard issued by the National
Information Standards Organization (Z39.48–1984).

10   9   8   7   6   5   4   3   2   1

For Alex and Auden, Mom and Dad
—J

For everyone who has supported me
—T

Contents

Chapter 9—Display in a Box (*Cont.*)

Acknowledgments

We would like to thank the Denver Public Library and specifically Beth Elder who had the foresight to bring merchandising to our library. Thank you to Cori Jackamore who also had the vision and then let us "run with it." Thank you to our families, friends, colleagues, and supervisors who were all very supportive during the writing process. Thank you to our colleagues near and far who have the same passion for merchandising and are always willing to think outside the box and share ideas. Thank you to the libraries who shared photographs: Arapahoe Library District, Denver Public Library, Jefferson County Public Library, and Saxton B. Little Free Public Library. A special thank you to the businesses who allowed us to take photographs or shared photographs with us: api(+)—Juan F. Romero, AIA, NCARB, President and CEO, and Thomas Henken, VP and Director of Design; The Complete Gourmet; Demco Inc.; Fancy Tiger; J.Jill; K.M. Concessions; SmartDraw.com; The Tattered Cover; Vitamin Cottage; and The Watermark. Thank you to Renee Chappelle of Renee Chappelle & Associates who gave us a lot of insight and to Merci Laurie for the laptop "rental." Last but not least, we thank our editor Barbara Ittner, who believed in the project.

Introduction: Merchandising

This book is the culmination of more than thirty years of combined retail and library experience of its authors. Trish brings more than fifteen years of retail experience with many companies. Along with customer service, she has merchandised products, designed and executed displays, and set up new store locations. Jenny has been a librarian for more than fifteen years. Her charge at the opening of the Schlessman Family Branch of the Denver Public Library was to try this new thing: "library merchandising."

When we met, we both recognized the usefulness of merchandising and the success created when these principles are applied to libraries. After giving numerous presentations on library merchandising, we decided to put all our information and research into one volume. We were also surprised and pleased to find that the topic of library merchandising appeared in library literature as early as the 1970s. Now we add retail literature and know-how to the mix to create a unique and handy source for you to consult when merchandising your collection. Our intention is to demonstrate these proven retail techniques to promote your collections through enticing experiences and to help you create an identity for your library. Both, in turn, will build customer and community loyalty.

**Libraries are evolving toward a more contemporary approach to usage.
Arapahoe Library District, Colorado.**

NOT THE FIRST, NOR THE LAST

As stated earlier, library merchandising has been studied and practiced for many, many years. Librarians literally throughout the world are merchandising on a daily basis whether they formally use the phrase *merchandising* or not. Many libraries and librarians have made great strides in this field by publishing articles, speaking, consulting, and sharing their knowledge, expertise, and ideas. We are by no means the first nor the only experts in library merchandising, but rather the scribes that have collated together retail knowledge and library practices. We are proud of our work in this field and encourage you to share and publish in this area as well. The bottom line for all of us is serving the public. Unlike the retail world, which must be concerned with its competition, we can afford to share the wealth so that all may benefit. Library merchandising isn't a trade secret. It just needs to be a given standard.

THE DEFINITIONS

The *Webster's Tenth New Collegiate Dictionary* defines merchandising as "to promote the sale of, as by advertising." A current retail text states "display and visual merchandising—however you break it up—is about presenting a product and any supporting material in the best possible manner."[1] Simply put, it is the methodical, artistic use of space to promote a product. *Merchandising* and *display* are often used synonymously, but they are in fact distinct from each other. "Visual merchandising is showing product in a way that motivates customers to buy. Display is a staged three-dimensional environment that creates an opportunity for customers to experience the product themselves."[2]

Retail companies have always used merchandising and displays to promote their identity, increase sales, and create a loyal customer base. They utilize all five senses to entertain the customer and keep them coming back for more. It is lovely to walk into Williams-Sonoma and smell the delicious fresh baked pumpkin bread. If you're a GAP or J.Jill shopper, those neatly folded T-shirts in the latest colors are irresistible. Waterfall soundtracks lull you through the Nature Company. Wal-Mart's bold "roll-back" price signs beckon you to look. Krispy Kreme lights up a sign to announce fresh-from-the-oven doughnuts. How many senses greet your library customers?

Folded sweaters. Courtesy of J.Jill.

WHO ME?

Although this book is primarily focused on public libraries, others, including special, school, and academic libraries, can benefit from these proven retail techniques. Even if you have a small or noncirculating collection, getting your materials to advertise themselves will in the end bring your customers to the collection more quickly and easily. Merchandising doesn't dictate what you put in your collection. Merchandising aids the collection you currently have.

TO RETAIL OR NOT TO RETAIL

Why should a library use merchandising when we are not selling a product? In actuality, we are selling our products. Our services may seem free, but the taxpayers, the local government, an institution, or a corporation supports them. The library's goal is to make itself as inviting to the community as possible while still remaining the democratic institution of learning that makes us so proud.

**Customers want libraries to offer current materials in various formats.
Schlessman Family Branch, Denver Public Library, Colorado.**

Traditionally, there has been a lot of resistance to merchandising in libraries. Our purpose is not to disregard our lofty ideals of higher learning by suggesting your library become a retail store. Nor do we suggest that you disassemble the uniqueness of your collection or abandon your careful cataloging. A groundbreaking article on library merchandising puts it best,

> the direction in which we would move is unfamiliar and not so dignified as perhaps we would like it to be.[3]

Library patrons have evolved, and public libraries need to cater to them. Information is so readily available now that the library no longer holds the corner on the market. We are no longer the only purveyors of knowledge, and to draw in our customers, we end up offering all kinds of things to all kinds of people: Internet access, multimedia, free classes, story times, musical programs—the list goes on. While promoting information and education, we need to find the balance between our roles as institutes of information and learning and that of entertainment center. One inexpensive and available way to turn back attention to our goal is to return the focus to our collections in an enlivened, fun way.

Throughout this book we ask a lot of questions that only you can answer for your library. We hope the questions and answers serve as a guide and jumping-off point from which to give you inspiration. With the guidelines that are given in later chapters and your personal creativity, your collections can shine with dynamic merchandising.

A CUSTOMER WALKS IN THE DOOR ...

Libraries can be daunting to the first-time visitor. They can be massive and imposing buildings, sometimes decades (or even centuries) old. Usually the first thing patrons see upon entering a library is a sterile service desk. Rows upon rows of shelves seem like an endless maze, and any classification system is a poor navigator to the uninitiated. If libraries want to thrive alongside the physical and virtual retailers, then we must use the proven technique of merchandising to help users find the materials they want or need. A high percentage of library patrons find materials by browsing. Merchandising helps focus customer attention in what could easily be a confusing environment.

This branch's "power wall" highlights its collection.
Jefferson County Public Library, Colorado.

Merchandising can entice customers inside and direct them throughout your library. It can also establish your brand and advertise programs or events. Rearranging items will spark your customers' interest and keep them coming back to see what's new. Presenting your collection to its best possible advantage also increases its value and makes for an entertaining experience. Most of all, merchandising will increase your circulation by bringing forth from your collection. The Schlessman Family Branch of the Denver Public Library has a collection of 98,000, yet it consistently circulates 80 to 90 percent of the circulation as the Denver Public Library's Central location, which has a circulating collection of more than 700,000. The circulation stays this high because the collection is consistently being highlighted with good merchandising and displays.

FOR THE LOVE OF A GOOD BOOK

To increase your circulation, you must attach value to your collections. Most, if not all, of us are in this field because of our love and devotion to the written word, and we long to share this emotional attachment with our customers. Retailers are experts at this. They get us crying at car commercials and drinking a beverage because they pull our heartstrings. The Disney Corporation, for example, has instilled emotional branding within its customers. Parents have memories of visiting the Disney parks and watching Disney movies as children. Because of the happy, nostalgic memories attached to this brand, they bring their children to the same parks and share their love of Disney's classic films with their children, not to mention purchase all the Disney products available.

The same can be said for libraries. Many customers remember how much they loved the library when they were younger, and they look forward to bringing their own children to the library. They wax nostalgic about the summer reading programs and their favorite librarians, but let's not forget the books.

Brand image creator and head of Desgrippes Gobé, Marc Gobé, said,

> Books have personalities, they're exciting, they're sulphurous, they're dangerous. Books have always been attached with emotions and are the most emotionally transforming things.[4]

Libraries understand the emotional impact of a good book. Gobé adds that

> bookstores should crank up the emotional interaction between people and the product. Books can be absolutely essential in defining a customer, in stimulating them, driving them to new ideas, expressing who they are. Books define people the way clothes and fragrances and shoes do.[5]

When you create this emotional connection to your collections and your library through merchandising, you ensure that your services will be appreciated and needed for generations to come.

A banned books display showcases the anticensorship movement. Schlessman Family Branch, Denver Public Library, Colorado.

RETAIL GOES LIBRARY

The bookstore industry has recognized customers' preference for library style and has incorporated many of our services to their benefit. Think of the last time you were in one of the larger retail bookstores. There were probably a multitude of customers browsing the shelves and reading. There may have been a children's area with colorful murals of literary characters and a theatrical stage for story times. Bookstores sponsor author readings and book signings. Even the buildings look like well-established libraries with their dark wooden shelves, overstuffed chairs, and reading tables. They have service desks where staff members can look up titles for customers and request new ones. Even online booksellers now allow you to preview a book before buying, offer staff and customer reviews, and further reading suggestions.

Even though booksellers have realized the importance of our style and use it to their advantage, they are still unable to attach that emotional branding that a library can. How many of you have misty-eyed memories of a bookstore?

Many booksellers utilize the "library look." The Tattered Cover, Denver, Colorado.

LET THE MERCHANDISING BEGIN

Library merchandising isn't just putting a book on a display table. Library merchandising is showcasing your entire collection in the most appealing and organized manner possible with an artistic eye for detail. This is accomplished through thoughtful merchandise selection and placement, appealing displays, and housekeeping.

As two crafty gals ourselves, we cannot stress enough the difference between *handmade* and *homemade*—handmade being artistic and classy while homemade falls short of either of these. The staff doing the merchandising needs to "get it" and be artistic. Merchandising of your collection is a serious undertaking and requires commitment. Although it isn't brain surgery and no one will get hurt with a bad display, lack of artistic flare, homemade signs, and empty spaces will advertise ineptness. Like musical improvisation, you first need a solid foundation of music theory. Once you have that, you can create your own tunes. The same can be applied for merchandising. Once you know the basics, you can create something uniquely yours.

You must be dedicated to trying new things, and you must like change. Remember, you are the driving force behind your collection when you purchase, process, shelve, and maintain it. The part that is usually missed is the dynamic way in which you merchandise your collection. The collection should always be up for an adventure and never be static. Your customers will thank you, and you will see library visits and circulation rise.

We can take a lesson from Starbucks' "Surprise & Delight" principle. Everyone has the basic ingredients, but they have that "extra *something* that differentiates them from their competition and builds brand loyalty."[6]

Library merchandising is our way to "surprise and delight" and offer that *something* that has high returns in customer satisfaction.

FACE-OUT ASSIGNMENTS

- What does merchandising mean to you?
- Why do you want to merchandise? What will be the outcome?
- Do you want to expose your customers to your materials?
- Do you want to increase your circulation?
- What are merchandising roadblocks you foresee personally and for your location?

NOTES

1. Tucker, Johnny. *Design, Display and Visual Merchandising*. Mies, Switzerland: RotoVision SA, 2003. 160p. $30. ISBN 2-88046-729-2.

2. Chappell, Rene. "Who Is Going to Create My Displays?" *Gourmet Retailer* (August 2001): 222.

3. Green, Sylvia A. "Merchandising Techniques and Libraries." *School Library Journal* (September 1981): 35–39.

4. Gobe, Marc. "Books Are So Emotional; Why Aren't Stores?" http://news.shelf-awareness.com (accessed February 26, 2007).

5. Ibid.

6. Michelli, Joseph A. *The Starbucks Experience: 5 Principles for Turning Ordinary into Extraordinary*. New York: McGraw Hill, 2007. 208p. $21.95. ISBN 978-0-07-147784-0.

Can you distinguish the bookstore from the library? The Tattered Cover, Denver, Colorado (this page), and Arapahoe Library District, Colorado (at right).

FURTHER READING

Baker, S. L. "The Display Phenomenon: An Exploration into Factors Causing the Increased Circulation of Displayed Books." *The Library Quarterly* 56, no. 3 (July 1986).

Baker, S. L. *The Responsive Public Library: How to Develop and Market a Winning Collection,* 2nd ed. Englewood, CO: Libraries Unlimited, 2002. 364p. $50. ISBN 1-56308-648-4.

Bernstein, Joan. "Merchandising the Library." *Library Journal* 131, no. 5 (March 15, 2006): 237–257.

Geary, Donna. "Curb Appeal: Developing a Powerful Store Image." http://www.impactvisual.com/publications/publications_curb_appeal.pp (accessed September 16, 2007).

Gerber, Michele. "Creative Merchandising: Insiders Insights from Retail Architect Jerome Schmider." *License!* 27, no. 5 (June 2004): 168–172.

Godhor, Herbert. "The Effect of Prime Display Location on Public Library Circulation of Selected Adult Titles." *The Library Quarterly* 42, no. 4 (October 1972): 371–389.

Godhor, Herbert. "Experimental Effects on the Choice of Books Borrowed by Public Library Adult Patrons." *The Library Quarterly* 51, no. 3 (1981): 263–268.

Latham, John R. " 'Stack 'em High, Sell 'em Cheap': Not Just for Retail Superstores." *Information Outlook* 11, no. 6 (June 2007): 92.

McIntosh, Melanie. "Attracting Customers: Steps to Getting More Shoppers in the Door." http://www.inspire.bc.ca (accessed August 7, 2007).

Merchandising Strategies: Manual. Towson, MD: Library Video Network, 2005. 10p. ISBN 1566410754.

Mittelstaedt, Robert. "Shopping Behavior and Retail Merchandising Strategies." *Journal of Business Research* 21, no. 3 (November 1990): 243–258.

South Jersey Regional Library Cooperative, "Trading Space: Reinventing the Library Environment." http://www.sjrlc.org/tradingspaces/index.shtml (accessed September 12, 2006).

Stone, Kenneth E. *Competing with the Retail Giants: How to Survive in the New Retail Landscape.* New York: Wiley, 2005. 259p. $110. ISBN 0471054402.

Woodward, Jeannette A. *Creating the Customer-Driven Library: Building on the Bookstore Model.* Chicago: American Library Association, 2005. 234p. $38. ISBN 0838908888.

1

Understanding Your Customer

HIT YOUR TARGET

The first step in successful merchandising is to understand how your location and facility are currently being used. This is done through knowing your target customers and how your traffic flows. Although merchandising can certainly bring notice to overlooked items, there is no point in advertising what no one wants. Retail stores strive to appeal to a broad range of customers, but they still have a target customer to whom they are catering. They attract this target customer through store decor, product, merchandising and staff. Retail expert Melanie McIntosh stresses that retailers who want to appeal to everyone get "a watered-down store identity and experience that doesn't appeal to anyone."[1] She states, "Knowing who your customers are and what they are passionate about is crucial for you to learn to understand what they need and want."[2]

This principle is clearly demonstrated by two stores within the same company. Urban Outfitters is targeting the eighteen to thirty-year-old, urban-minded young adult who follows the current trends, whereas Anthropologie's customer is the sophisticated and contemporary thirty- to forty-five-year-old woman focused on career, family, and home.[3] Both are part of the same company and want to appeal to everyone, but each is tailored to attract a particular customer. Think about your favorite store, and what it is that initially makes you want to shop there. Is it the convenient location, the range of products, the like-minded staff? Using your experience as a customer is a great way to better understand your library's customers.

1

IN YOUR NEIGHBORHOOD

To quote Mr. Rogers, "Who are the people in your neighborhood?" Libraries are set up for the general public, but each location tends to attract a certain clientele depending on the neighborhood's demographics and the services offered.

- Are you a large urban library or a small suburban one?
- Are you the only library or one of many in a district?
- Are you in a new neighborhood or an established one?
- Is there a K–12 school or institution of higher learning nearby?
- What is the socioeconomic makeup of your area?

Knowing who your neighbors are is the first step in understanding your customers. Just like retailers, we want to have a general appeal to draw in new customers, but because birds of a feather flock together, chances are you will have a particular type of customer who uses your library more frequently than others. Of course, you don't want to single out or neglect anyone, but you can put some emphasis on your collection for that common denominator.

This bicycling display ties into a community event. Schlessman Family Branch, Denver Public Library, Colorado.

There is a new trend in libraries to focus locations on certain clientele or products. The Douglas County Libraries in Colorado have designated two branches as "Neighborhood Branches." These locations focus on popular materials and merchandising of the entire collection. This was determined by the actual square footage of the locations rather than demographics.[4] In the Denver Public Library, the branches are now focused on certain clientele and carry materials and programs for that audience: Family, Contemporary, Children's, and Learning & Language. In an e-mail to the authors, Beth Elder, former Director of Planning for Denver Public Library, said "Denver's unique demographics created several distinct patterns of library use. The patterns of use evolved into different branch service styles that were then distributed throughout the City, mostly by dominant user patterns. Geography was considered in the distribution of the styles to maximize the possibility [that] customers could choose from a variety of service styles in proximity to their home."[5]

WHO GOES THERE?

Customers sometimes tell us that their time is very valuable to them and they would rather "pay for the convenience" of a bookstore or an online retailer. Why would they pay for something that they can borrow for free? What is it about a library that makes it less convenient? Well, for starters, many customers are unfamiliar with the classification system used and therefore don't know where to begin in a library. Another obstacle is that the book they want could be right there in front of them, but they can't see the title because it's buried under a call number label. Sometimes the dust jacket is too dirty for them to even read the title. Bookstore products are brand new, while ours can be years old and well worn, which can turn off many customers. Library shelves can be up to six feet tall, which presents a problem if the customer is short. Or maybe the item is on the bottom shelf, and it's too difficult for the customer to bend over. We will address some of these housekeeping issues in detail later in the book, but this gives you an idea of some of the challenges and inconveniences patrons face at the library.

**Signs within the stacks are a great navigational aid.
Arapahoe County Library District, Colorado.**

Once you know who your customers are, you can begin to make changes to accommodate them. Retailers hold focus groups and utilize market research to determine their target customer's wants and needs. Libraries keep up with community demographics and solicit feedback from their constituents. Of course, both groups look at their bottom line, of either sales or circulation, to determine success. Libraries work within certain limits and constraints (such as budgets), but by observing and listening to your customer, you can determine how to make small changes that will have a big impact on their library experience. Although you don't want to forget that niche customer, you do want to offer up what is being sought most. Knowing how your customers use your library helps avoid making mistakes such as placing a children's book display next to a study room. Here are some questions to consider when determining your customer base.

- What is the age range of your customers?
- What is the purpose of their visit?
- Are your customers new or long-time users?
- Are your customers self-sufficient, or do they need assistance?

As homework, visit your local bookseller. Pay attention to how you move through the store and what you are drawn to. What do you like or dislike? Are you able to find items easily, or do you need to ask for help? Do you want to get in and out right away, or do you find yourself lingering? Many people now see the bookstore as a way to spend an afternoon, even making it a neighborhood hangout. We want to recreate that type of community place that you find in these bookstores within our libraries.

Bookstores encourage customers to peruse their products by offering comfortable reading areas. The Tattered Cover, Denver, Colorado.

HOW DOES YOUR TRAFFIC FLOW?

Unfortunately, many older libraries were built not with the customer in mind, but with pragmatic storage as the main focus. Older libraries tend to be boxy rooms filled with rows of high, metal shelving. Yet newer branches aren't perfect either. While a lot of new libraries have been built to allow for merchandising, many of these display units are created with more of an architectural aesthetic in mind rather than functionality. And thought for mobility? Forget about it.

Now, don't despair. Whether you have an older, classic building or a newer, contemporary design, there are opportunities. The customers still travel the same general traffic pathways. A universal retail fact is that when a customer enters a store, they turn right and shop in a counterclockwise path.[6] Retailers want the customer to travel through the entire store and therefore lay out their fixtures along this path.

To determine your traffic flow, you need to draw a map of your branch. This doesn't have to be proportionately correct, but it does need to show your entrances/exits, collection, furniture, and service areas.

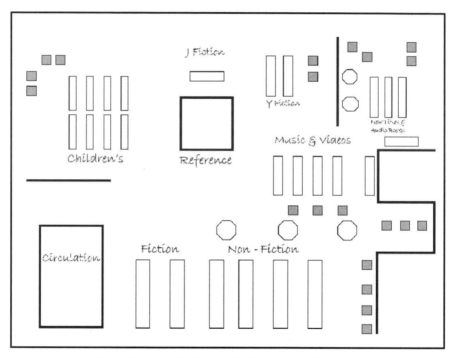

Branch map indicating collection and service areas.

Now trace the path of customers until you see a pattern emerging. Follow this checklist when evaluating your traffic path.

- What areas are receiving the most traffic?
- What is along the high-traffic areas?
- What is at the end destination of the high-traffic areas?
- What areas are being neglected?

- Do you have any "road blocks" such as furniture, walls, or public service desks?

- Is there a circular traffic flow throughout the library, or does the traffic flow into a corner?

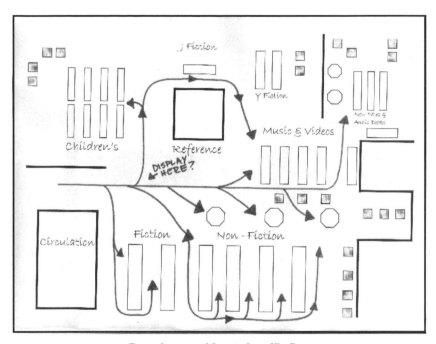

Branch map with noted traffic flow.

Once you see where your customer is traveling through your branch, you can begin to make some changes to better accommodate them. Even small moves can make a big difference in helping your customers find what they need.

Now ask yourself these important questions:

- What is drawing patrons inside in the first place?

    Look at your library's entrance from the outside and see through your customers' eyes. Can you see an inviting entryway, or does it look dreary, cluttered, or empty?

- What is leading them around your space?

    Do your clients move through your library strictly for service areas or do they browse with no set direction?

- When standing at the entrance, do you see parts of the collection or fixtures?

  Nothing is more of a turnoff than bland shelf ends. You don't want your library to look like a warehouse, so try angling your fixtures to show off the materials. This is also a good reason to have a display at the entrance that your patrons see as soon as they walk in the door.

- Do you need to move some furniture to open up a pathway?

  This can be one of the easiest moves to make. Are your reading desks in a high traffic area? Can you move them to a quieter area, more conducive to concentration? Consider creating "purpose areas" or zones for your library. For example open areas with desk space for WiFi and computer use separate from quiet reading of new magazines separate from listening to music at music stations separate from the information desk. All these activities bring a variety of noises.

- Is it difficult for a customer to find particular areas or items?

  If a large percentage of your customers ask where to find something, that is a good indicator that you need to give it more visual prominence. Can you avoid using the top and bottom shelves or use them only for overstock?

Knowing your traffic flow can also help you determine where to locate your displays. You want your displays to be advertising stops along this path starting at the entrance and ending up at the checkout desk with an entertaining journey along the way.

LETTUCE LESSONS

Supermarkets today have a set path for you to follow whether you know it or not. In recent years Safeway grocery stores have rolled out their "Lifestyle" stores "that sell solutions to shoppers, rather than just single items."[7] There may be a display of pie tins in the produce section to encourage you to head to the baking aisle after picking up some apples. They will also have get-well cards by the pharmacy, which will make you think of flowers as well. Charcoal in the meat department brings to mind the paper plates in the paper goods aisle. "It actually pulls you from merchandise table to merchandise table."[8] And it is clearly working: "the Lifestyle format [has] been the primary driver of Safeway's increased same-store growth."[9]

Roadblocks in your library can discourage customer use. Schlessman Family Branch, Denver Public Library.

Clear paths will keep your customer "shopping the floor." Schlessman Family Branch, Denver Public Library.

AT THE END OF THE DAY

All this having been said, you don't want to overwhelm the patron with too much signage and too many fixtures. After all, libraries are known for efficient organization, not the chaos of a bargain basement store. We want our customers to come in, spend as much or as little time as they prefer, and leave with what they wanted and maybe something they didn't know they wanted. How can the library be an efficient part of your customer's day? Make your map, find the traffic patterns, and make your changes. As in the retail world, things change. Time of year, population growth or loss, and budgets can all affect your traffic flow. Be nimble enough to go with the flow.

FACE-OUT ASSIGNMENTS

- Visit your local bookstore and pay attention to your shopping experience. What did you like the most? The least? Was it easy to find what you needed?

- Who are your "common denominator" customers, and what do they need most? Evaluate their needs and decide what changes you can make to accommodate them.

- Determine your traffic flow by making a map and watching your customers. Make any moves necessary to create your traffic path from the entrance to the checkout desk.

- Visit the store for which you would most like to receive a $100 gift card. What do you see immediately upon entering? Do the displays encourage you to move from on to another? What is the traffic flow you are following in the store?

NOTES

1. McIntosh, Melanie. "Attracting Customers: Steps to Getting More Shoppers in the Door." http://www.inspire.bc.ca (accessed August 7, 2007).

2. Ibid.

3. Urban Outfitters, Inc. "Brand Profiles." http://wurbanoutfiittersinc. com/profile/ (accessed April 3, 2007).

4. James LaRue (Director, Douglas County Libraries), e-mail message to authors, September 13, 2007.

5. Beth Elder (former Director of Planning, Denver Public Library), e-mail message to authors, September 19, 2007.

6. "Buy/Merchandising Advice—Plan Store Layout Changes Carefully." *Extra Touch Online* (July 2002): 2.

7. DiNardo, Anne, "Safeway Lifestyle Store." May 9, 2005. http://www.visualstore.com/index.php/channel/27/id/9011 (accessed March 18, 2007).

8. Ibid.

9. Mara, Janis. "Safeway's 'Lifestyle' Delivers Nice Returns Safeway Quarter Profit." *Oakland Tribune*, October 13, 2006.

FURTHER READING

"Combining a Decorative Touch with Historical Perspective." *Hardware Retailing* 196, no. 6 (December 2007): 22.

Murray, Raphel. "Keep Your Customers on the Path to Purchase." *Art Business News* 30, no. 7 (July 2003): 30.

Perry, Phillip M. "Put Some 'Pop' into Your Bottom Line." *American Nurseryman* 181, no. 12 (June 15, 1995): 44–48.

Trade Shows. *Gourmet Retailer* 24, no. 8 (August 2004): 174.

2

Secrets of the Trade

There are two types of merchandising that translate effectively into a library setting. One is *collection presentation standards* or *CPS,* which incorporates presentation techniques you can do within the shelving run to create interest. The other is a *display,* which is a stand-alone, themed arrangement that can act as a signpost or advertising teaser. This chapter focuses on CPS. Displays are discussed in the next two chapters.

COLLECTION PRESENTATION STANDARDS (CPS)

One of the greatest differences between a bookstore and a library is merchandise storage. A bookstore wants their merchandise to be temporarily stored on their shelf as a limited collection based on the popularity of a title. It does a bookstore no good to have an unwanted title taking up valuable real estate. A library, on the other hand, acts as an archive and customers expect a depth of collection. Which means libraries need to store their merchandise in the most space-efficient way possible, hence the traditional spine-out method. One of the ways to combat any lack of storage space is to keep the collection moving. Just think how much space it would take to house your entire collection at once! To keep the collection moving, you need to promote it. CPS is necessary for promoting your older collection, and following these standards ensures that your shelved collection is attractive and accessible. CPS works for print as well as for audio-visual titles. All of your staff should be trained to shelve materials within these standards. Once implemented, CPS is easy to maintain.

There are several principles and techniques that should be considered when you implement CPS standards: the crescent, front it, face out, right hand, and your own customized guidelines.

The Crescent

Within the run, use a "crescent," which is few to no books on the top and bottom shelves and more in the middle. Customers shop between eye and waist level, this is why the popular name-brand items are on the middle shelves at the grocery store. Placing more of your collection within this shopping zone will capitalize on your customers' preexisting shopping habits. The crescent also prevents injuries from excessive stooping or items falling from above. Try to avoid putting adult titles on the bottom shelves and children's titles on the top shelves. They are the least accessible shelves for these particular customers. Instead, use these areas for oversized items. You may notice in retail establishments that overstock items are kept up high or down low.

The crescent shape ensures the most material is accessible.
Schlessman Family Branch, Denver Public Library, Colorado.

Front It

How many times have you stretched to reach that last can of green beans at the back of the top shelf? Don't make your customer work for that book; your collection needs to be front and center. Front your materials by pulling them to the edge of the shelf for a clean line and easy-to-read call number. This also applies to items on a table or in a display. Pull them as close to the customer as you can. If your oversized books stick out too far, consider laying them flat and spine out on the bottom shelf, or putting them in holders at the end of the shelf. Incorporate as much of your collection together to provide one-stop shopping.

Compare the clean lines of materials fronted versus not fronted.
Jefferson County Public Library, Colorado.

Let's Face It

Think about the last time you purchased wine. Were you persuaded to purchase based on the label? Customers do judge books by their covers, and that is motivation enough to get the cover seen.

Colorful labels vie for attention in a wine department. Auto Mercado de Oeste S.A., San Jose, Costa Rica. Courtesy api(+). Photo credit: Rocio Escobar, San Jose, Costa Rica.

To showcase those covers, face out multiple copies within the run. It is best to use hardbound titles rather than paperback for this. Simply take the copies, turn them cover out and tighten up the row. Besides being a great attention getter, this can free up space if you have many copies of a title. If your collection is small, facing out more than one title in a row can also fill up the shelf by eliminating space at the end of the row. You can also feature a title or two by placing them face out at the end of the shelf. When doing this, choose a title from within the run on that particular shelf to accommodate reshelving and locating. Make sure your faced-out copies are in good condition—with bright, striking covers, if possible. Avoid stacking books flat on the shelf, spine out. This does not put focus on the covers, which is what you want to feature. Publishers spend time and money on creating eye-catching covers, so use them to your advantage. We guarantee the faced-out titles will be the fast movers.

Covers offer wonderful, free artwork to help "sell" the collection. Schlessman Family Branch, Denver Public Library, Colorado.

You're Right

Another universal retail fact is that customers shop with their right hands. Check out the mug display at Crate and Barrel. All the handles are faced for your right hand. Hangers are hung like a question mark to be taken with the right hand. Books prove to be difficult in this regard because they are designed from left to right. Try to take a book from the shelf with your right hand and read the cover. It's pretty awkward right? You had to switch hands or flip it around, didn't you? We generally take books from a shelf with our left hand so we can see the cover and open them. Spine out shelving does not accommodate right-handed shopping. This is another reason to face out copies for your customer.

Retailers stock merchandise so it is accessible to the "right shopping" customer. Fancy Tiger, Denver, Colorado.

Uniquely Yours

The four standards just described need to be combined with what standards you set for your own location. Colorado's Arapahoe Library District spells out merchandising standards for their libraries in a well-articulated document, "Merchandising for Impact: Merchandising Guidelines at Arapahoe Library District," which includes photographs.

Before: Picture books in the Arapahoe Library District, Colorado.

Walk the floor of your library and look at the collection as the customer sees it. Take photographs to review with other staff. Viewing photographs can really illustrate what is being seen. Devise standards that incorporate CPS.

THE BIG BANG

CPS requires little effort, but it gives a big visual impact to your collection. When shelving titles in a series, keep them in numerical order. To assist with location, alphabetize fiction and nonfiction by title, after author or classification number. Train your shelvers to maintain CPS when reshelving by fronting, shelf reading, and facing out the shelf to which they are returning a title. It takes just a few moments and helps guarantee that every shelf gets straightened throughout the day. Every morning, bright and early, you will find staff in supermarkets restocking, bringing items to the edge, and facing out labels. Take your cue from retail's attention to detail.

After: three books per section. Arapahoe Library District, Colorado.

Before: Business display, Arapahoe Library District, Colorado.

After: Business display made more accessible by not stacking.
Arapahoe Library District, Colorado.

Traditional shelving utilizing CPS will create excitement for your collection.
Schlessman Family Branch, Denver Public Library, Colorado.

Vitamin Cottage (Denver, Colorado) shelves ready for customers.

PLEASE COME AGAIN

Bookmarks are a great way to feature book lists and bibliographies. These can be a promotional giveaway item much like a "free gift with purchase." Bookmarks are something that the library customer will use with your merchandise and that cost you very little to produce. Library patrons frequently ask for titles or authors similar to the ones they already enjoy. By providing them with a suggested reading, viewing, or listening list, you virtually guarantee return visits from your customers. Feature bookmarks in your books and audiovisual materials, rather than laying them flat on a table, and use them in CPS and displays. For CPS, create some read-alike lists for popular authors, such as "If you like Jodi Picoult, then try …" Pick a couple of popular authors you want to feature, and put the bookmarks in the books on the shelves. This technique serves two purposes. First, the bookmarks grab your customer's attention when they are browsing the fiction or nonfiction, just like the blinking coupon dispensers in the grocery store. Second, they give your customer a reason to come back by providing them with other authors or subject-related titles they might like. With displays, create a bibliography of themed titles and put them inside the library items. Bookmarks can also promote your library services and upcoming community events. Try a bookmark about the library's homebound services in your large print titles or computer classes in your computer manuals.

FACE-OUT ASSIGNMENTS

- Evaluate your CPS. Walk up and down every row and around every fixture.
- Can you see a crescent shape?
- Are items faced out?
- Are items brought to the edge?
- Are titles in alphabetical or numerical order?
- Set standards for you library.
- Choose an author to feature and create read-alike bookmarks.

Eye-catching bookmarks in the fiction collection are surefire attention-getters.
Schlessman Family Branch, Denver Public Library, Colorado.

FURTHER READING

Long, Sarah P. "The Effect of Face-Front Book Display in a Public Library." *North Carolina Libraries* 45, no. 3 (Fall 1987): 150–153.

"Merchandising the Collection: Trading Spaces Demonstration Project, Mount Laurel Library, Staff Walk-Through #1 Notes—July 2003." Mount Laurel Library, 2004. http://www.mtlaurel.lib.nj.us (accessed September 19, 2007).

3

Display Zones

LOCATION, LOCATION, LOCATION

Displays are your changeable, themed promotions and an opportunity to show your creative talents. Every retailer uses displays, and they are a wonderful way to inject some color and fun into your library. Stroll you local mall and look at all the store windows that beckon you in. You'll see examples all around you of awesome merchandising and display. Anthropologie "is one retailer that has masterminded the art of merchandising, which is not so much about peddling wares as it is about telling a good story."[1]

What story do you want to tell?

There are eight key areas, or zones as they are referred to in retail, where a display can focus attention and advertise what your library has to offer.

- Entry

- New Titles

- Fiction

- Nonfiction

- Media

- Teens

- Children

- Point of Check Out (POCO)

25

Entry Display

If you can only have one display, it should be an entry display. Retail stores always have an entry display, whether it's a window display or a fixture right inside the doors. Imagine you were given a $100 gift card to your favorite store. What is at the entryway of this store that draws you inside?

Retailers know the importance of a great first impression.
The Watermark, Denver, Colorado.

The entry is where the customer pauses to look around, and it's your first opportunity to showcase your library and its collection. One hundred percent of walk-in customers come into the first few feet of your library, usually to a service desk. Your entry display can draw them in further and reinforce their decision to spend time at the library. Entry displays should feature a current topic and represent a veritable smorgasbord of your collection. Here is a good place to promote the current holiday or community event. By featuring items from all departments (books, periodicals, children's, young adult, languages, audio, visual, etc.), you give the customer a taste of all that the library has to offer. In retail, this is known as cross-merchandising, or adjacencies, which encourages add-on sales.

An entry display can be used as a promotional teaser to encourage return visits. Schlessman Family Branch, Denver Public Library, Colorado.

Your entry display always needs to be changing and evolving. Target stores brilliantly introduced the "One Spot"—bins and bins of items for a dollar or two. "This strategy works because once customers are ready to buy something—anything—they are ready to buy something else. They have gone from saying 'I'm just looking' to thinking 'what else do they have that I can buy?' "[2] By the same token, what customers see upon entering your library can be detrimental if there isn't something to pique their interest.

What is the first thing you see upon entering your library?

Newbies

New titles are your hot, high-end merchandise, and this should be your second most important display. Your new titles are what keep your customers coming back again and again. Think of the people who rush out to get the newest toy or see the latest film. This is an area that can sell itself if presented in an accessible, appealing way. One successful way to promote this section is to have some new materials near the front, but the rest toward the back of your branch. After all, you don't want to give up all of your good stuff at once.

Why is the clearance section at the back of a retail store? This is to get you to walk through the store *twice* to get the things you want most. Maybe you'll see something else along the way you wouldn't have noticed before. Remember your traffic flow; you want the customer to see the entire library.

New titles are a hot commodity when merchandised to their full potential. Schlessman Family Branch, Denver Public Library, Colorado.

Fiction and Nonfiction

Fiction lends itself to great themes by genres, subgenres, and available prolific writers. Here is your opportunity to introduce your customers to new authors as well as titles by their favorites. On the flip side, nonfiction has much to offer that might have otherwise gone unread. There are a lot of great nonfiction titles that read like fiction. (Sounds like a display theme.) In fact, nonfiction is hot right now and "is the great new frontier of readers' advisory."[3] Nonfiction has been on an upswing since the new millennium with many nonfiction titles topping the best-sellers list. Readers nowadays are more likely to have the latest celebrity memoir than a novel. Reality television shows, documentaries, and films based on true stories have also been steadily gaining popularity. Pop culture commentator and essayist Chuck Klosterman calls it the "Rise of the Real."[4] Sarah Statz Cords talks at length about why the promotion of nonfiction is so important in her book *The Real Story: A Guide to Nonfiction Reading Interests* (Libraries Unlimited, 2006). This increased interest in real stories makes it all the more important to merchandise your nonfiction collection.

When you enter a bookstore or a library, you will see the fiction section divided into its many genres such as science fiction, fantasy, romance, western, and mystery. These genre divisions and prolific authors make it rather easy to create a fiction display. On the other side of the bookstore aisle, you will also see the nonfiction titles arranged by subject. Travel, business, cooking, and self-help are all showcased to draw the customer to the desired topic. Not so in the library, where nonfiction is generally spine-out on endless rows of shelves cataloged according to a system that is unfamiliar to most readers. Nonfiction can also be a challenge because many titles could be cataloged under many different headings. Featuring many titles by the same authors, fiction makes it easy for customers to find something that interests them, and it gives you an opportunity to show the reader new authors. With a few exceptions such as chefs and their cookbooks, nonfiction authors don't write as many books as fiction authors do. Utilizing CPS and a few creative displays can draw customers into the stacks and help promote your older collection. Luckily, many online tools are now available to help with suggested nonfiction reading. *The Reader's Advisor Online* (from Libraries Unlimited) and *Non-Fiction Connection* (from Bowker) can be used to find ideas for nonfiction display themes. Your nonfiction collection is also a place to tie into community events or museum exhibits. By promoting these areas, you can increase your older collection's circulation. Merchandise within the run by facing out multiple copies to showcase their beautiful covers. Show off those covers rather than just rows and rows of spines to keep the customer shopping throughout the stacks. Even on traditional shelves, you can be creative. Just empty one shelf and build a mini-display area on it.

Displays can easily be done on traditional shelving. Smiley Branch, Denver Public Library, Colorado.

Media

The traditional stuff

We often think media can sell itself by the lone fact that we buy it. However, areas where audio books, DVDs, VHS, and electronic games are shelved can all benefit from a little extra exposure. These items look great next to their printed counterparts, which advertise the other available formats of your collection. Select fixtures and stands that show off the covers, and include media advisory bookmarks in these areas. Be sure to replace broken packaging to keep these items looking their best as well.

What's new?

New to libraries are eBook, eAudios, and eFlicks. How are you promoting them? Because they're totally electronic, there's nothing to display, right? Don't let this deter you—creative signage in the library, in your library newsletter, bookmarks, and on your Web site can be used to let customers know what's available. Just because customers download them to their own PDAs, MP3s, and laptops away from the library, doesn't mean you shouldn't be promoting these alongside the traditional hard copies.

Other Electronic Resources

Libraries pay big bucks for electronic resources and yet are sometimes disappointed that their uses aren't high. Print publicity materials for these resources and place them with their print counterparts to help advertise that you have other formats.

Advertising your electronic services alongside the hard copy will promote all you have to offer. Denver Public Library, Bear Valley Branch, Colorado.

Teens and Children

Young Adult and Children's collections need the same merchandising treatments as their adult counterparts. Sure, these areas see a lot of traffic during the summer reading programs, and book reports will help bring kids in during the school year. Yet there are so many other ways to look at your youth collections. Summer vacations are a great opportunity to promote youth audio titles for those long drives. Movies based on a book will create renewed interest in it, as will the last title in a series—Harry Potter anyone?

These teen titles are sure to be grabbed up. Central Branch, Denver Public Library, Colorado.

Fiction

When it comes to fiction, teens will rarely ask a librarian for suggested titles. More likely they will have a required reading list from their teacher and will depend on browsing and friends' recommendations for pleasure reading. Why not spark their interest with popular and catchy covers? Read-alike displays offer young readers direction after the last chapter in a series has ended. What about assigned reading? Get your hands on a copy of the local school's reading list and have a display ready. Another way to generate interest is to solicit teen reviews either in-house or from your Web site. Post the results on bookmarks tucked into the highlighted items. By treating the teen and children fiction areas with the same attention to merchandising as the adult fiction, you are showing that you value your younger customer while increasing circulation.

Nonfiction

A display is much more appealing to children than shelved materials.
Schlessman Family Branch, Denver Public Library, Colorado.

The same principles apply in youth and juvenile nonfiction as well. Here is a great opportunity to promote community events and school projects. Check out what exhibits your local museums will be showing. Chances are the schools will be studying these topics in class and making field trips to see these exhibits. Do you notice that your 500s are moving at a particular time of the year? It could be science fair time. Watch for these trends or check with your local schools to find out when certain subjects will be studied. You will be amazed at how your juvenile nonfiction collection moves with well-timed displays. What if your juvenile nonfiction doesn't circulate well? If the books have great content and appeal and good-looking covers, before weeding, pull the titles and create a display to give them a second opportunity.

A display of any subject can generate interest. Smoky Hills Library, Arapahoe Library District, Colorado.

POCO (Point of Check Out)

POCO is a great way to get that last item into your customer's hand. In retail this is called POP (point of purchase), POS (point of sales), or impulse purchases. Your customers are in line to check out, so why not give them something to browse while they wait? Think about the magazines you look through at the grocery store checkout. Chances are that your customer will take an item with them rather than put it back once they have it in their hands. And how cool is it that library "impulse purchases" are free?

**Who can resist the impulse items at the checkout counter?
Watermark, Denver, Colorado.**

POCO is also an excellent spot for a temporary merchandise push or if you have a small new title collection. Stack up that hot new title by the self-checkout and watch everyone grab a copy as they go! You could also feature staff recommendations at the circulation desk by having staff members each put out a title at their workstations. As these titles get snatched up, be prepared to restock quickly and always make sure whatever is at your POCO is neat and tidy.

A current magazine display at POCO mirrors the retail experience. Schlessman Family Branch, Denver Public Library, Colorado.

A new title is sure to be grabbed up by everyone. Schlessman Family Branch, Denver Public Library, Colorado.

LIBRARY DEPARTMENT STORE

The eight areas just described are key merchandising areas. However, don't overwhelm yourself by setting up more displays that you can handle. You don't need a display on every available surface. This will only make your library look cluttered, as well as making specific items hard to find. The objective is to focus attention on the different "departments" in your library and lead your customer to each one. If you are able to only have one or two displays, then have an entry and a new titles display, because these will give you the most bang for your buck.

THROW AWAY THE LOCK

When determining where to place your display, choose areas that your customers can get to easily. It is of the utmost importance that you do not lock up your materials in a glass display case or on a shelf behind a service desk. Materials locked in a case should be reserved for archives and museums. You want the customer to take the item. It's a well-known fact in retail that you have a better chance of making a sale if you get the product in the customer's hands. Even requiring the customer to ask for the item that is on display behind the service desk is a deterrent.

Of course, if you really want to include some titles in a locked display case, then color copy the cover and include a little sign saying, "Find Me in j398.2's" for example. Or better yet, take the glass doors off, throw away the lock and make those shelves accessible. The whole point of your collection is to allow your customer access.

OH DISPLAY CAN YOU SEE?

A display also needs to be seen from a distance by the most people possible. Displays catch your customers' eyes and draw them in. Ideally, you should be able to see each display from the main traffic areas, much like the end caps in the grocery store, so try to keep your fixtures on your traffic flow pathway. However, always be willing and able to change.

Our experiences have shown that slat wall fixtures located within the middle of the aisles limited the number of people who would see the display, instead of keeping them shopping in the stacks. Your location may prove different. We moved the fixtures to the ends of the aisles where they could be seen from the entrance, thereby increasing their advertising capabilities. Now they are pulling people into the stacks who might otherwise have never gone there.

Materials locked in a case will not increase your circulation.
Central Branch, Denver Public Library, Colorado.

A faraway display piques curiosity and draws the customer further along.
Bear Valley Branch, Denver Public Library, Colorado.

Bloom Supermarkets. Courtesy api(+). Photo credit:
Tim Buchman, Charlotte, North Carolina.

Follow the key area and traffic flow guidelines when selecting from preexisting fixtures, especially those fixtures in corners or rarely traveled areas. Don't overwhelm yourself by thinking every display unit has to have a themed display. You still need to be able to perform daily upkeep on your merchandising. Use these out-of-the-way areas as promotion space for library services or community events.

CPS and the choice of where to display your collection will have a profound impact on your circulation. If at first you don't succeed, be willing to change it up a bit. Our customers change and thus our traffic patterns change throughout the year and over time. By sticking with CPS and displays, you are presenting your collection in the best possible way.

FACE-OUT ASSIGNMENTS

- Assess your current display areas.
- How many displays do you currently have?
- How many would you ideally like to have?
- Can you maintain them?
- Do the display(s) draw your customers to them, or do customers stumble upon them?
- Is there any circulating material in your locked cases?

NOTES

1. "Design 100." *Metropolitan Home* (May 2007): 88.

2. Raphel, Murray. "Keeping Customers on the Path to Purchase." *Art Business News* (July 2003): 30.

3. Saricks, Joyce. "Taking on Nonfiction Reader's Advisory." *Booklist* (March 1, 2005): 1141.

4. Klosterman, Chuck. "Rise of the Real." *Esquire* (December 2004): 194.

FURTHER READING

Cords, Sarah Statz. *The Real Story: A Reading Guide to Nonfiction Reading Interests.* Westport, CT: Libraries Unlimited, 2006. 461p. ISBN 1591582830.

Folkmanis, Judy. "Making Puppet Sales Come Alive." *Playthings* 98, no. 2 (February 2000): 250.

Hutton, Eileen. "Audiobooks Deserve Marketing, Too." *Publishers Weekly* 252, no. 42 (October 24, 2005): 66.

Maas, John Michael. "The Display Dilemma." *Publishers Weekly* 250, no. 35 (September 1, 2003): 19–22.

Nichols, Mary Ann. *Merchandising Library Materials to Young Adults.* Englewood, CO: Libraries Unlimited, 2002. 187p. $44. ISBN 0313313822.

Tools of the Trade

FIXTURES AND FURNITURE

Now that you have selected your display locations from your traffic flow and customer needs, you need to decide which type of fixtures and furniture you will use for your displays.

Fixtures are a tough call as they must be totally functional, flexible, easy to use, adjustable, and most importantly, be all that without outshining the products. They should function much like the frame of a picture whereby you get to choose the frame you want, but if it takes away from the picture, you have totally missed its function.[1]

Fixture Options

We recommend two types of fixtures for library displays: various tables and the slat wall. These two types come in a variety of styles that, in our experience, have some pros and cons to take into consideration. It is important that you get the fixture that best fits your space and accommodates the number of titles you are able to display at any given time.

41

Tables

Bookstore tables have many merchandising features.
Schlessman Family Branch, Denver Public Library, Colorado.

"Bookstore" tables are great for entry and new-title displays. These tables are the workhorses for your displays because they can feature slat wall sides for faced out items, sides with adjustable shelving and multilevel flat surfaces. They can accommodate a medium to large quantity of titles, plus an optional prop or two, which helps the display look full at all times. Angle titles toward the traffic flow, so the customer can move around the table to see all sides.

**Nesting tables provide different heights for merchandising.
Denver Zoo. Courtesy of K.M. Concessions.**

Nesting tables are best if your display is against a wall so customers don't see the back of items. Each table can be slid out or in to accommodate the changing number of titles. If you use tablecloths, you can store extra stock underneath. These tables are less expensive than "bookstore" tables and are easier to move. Nesting tables work well with a small to medium quantity of titles.

Cubes

A stair-step cube arrangement for limited approach merchandising.
Arapahoe Library District.

If you don't have enough room to accommodate a large table, consider modular display cubes. Cubes can offer you the best of both worlds because they are lightweight and offer many arrangement possibilities. They can be stacked wedding-cake style to allow titles to be viewed from all sides, or stair stepped for viewing from one angle. Cubes generally come in 18- or 20-inch diameters, so they don't offer a lot of surface area or height. Six cubes will only give you five horizontal surfaces because the smaller ones cover up a large one. The more cubes you get, the more surface area and the more configurations. Again, be safety oriented and don't stack cubes too high.

A tiered cube arrangement for all-around merchandising.
Arapahoe Library District, Colorado.

Easels

**Wire and Plexiglas book easels. Schlessman Family Branch,
Denver Public Library, Colorado.**

Easels (or book stands) are one of the most important accessories available for table and shelf displays. Standing a book on its end eventually breaks the spine and the text block. Books are also more likely to fall over like dominoes when stood up in this manner. Adjustable easels can be used on display tables and with Collection Presentation Standards at the end of the run. Hinged wire easels offer more options over Plexiglas stands, because they are adjustable to accommodate multiple copies and large bound titles. However, Plexiglas stands work well for larger or heavier items.

Risers

Colorful boxes used as risers. Jefferson County Public Library, Colorado.

Lifts and levels are important for highlighting each title and for creating height, which means risers are a necessary addition to your toolbox. Risers can be purchased as wooden or clear Plexiglas boxes and come in a variety of sizes. Plexiglas risers can also be filled with a fun prop. Don't be discouraged if you don't have the budget to purchase risers. Get creative and use items like paint cans as risers for a 'Home Improvement' theme or popcorn tubs for "Movies from Books." Cardboard boxes of different sizes can be used as well. Wrap boxes in paper or place them under a tablecloth to give them a professional and sharp appearance. No matter what you use, make sure your riser is in excellent condition and kept it clean.

Creative risers are a great inexpensive alternative.
Schlessman Family Branch, Denver Public Library, Colorado.

Slat wall

Whereas tables accommodate a horizontal display, slat walls can be used for a vertical display. Slat wall fixtures can be used on walls, at free-standing kiosks, or as units within your shelves. A slat wall is made up of rows of boards with gaps between them. These gaps create a slot for hangers to support shelves or Plexiglas accessories. Library catalogs feature a plethora of options.

Slat wall accessories

There are many kinds of slat wall accessories that you can use, depending on where your fixture is located. These fixtures should be accessible to the customer, but they must also be safe. When using slat wall paneling on a wall or at the end of range shelving, avoid using a lot a shelves that a customer can bump. A single shelf placed up high can hold your props and sign, and make your vignette (see Chapter 5, "Anatomy of a Display") visible.

Slat wall. Bear Valley Branch, Denver Public Library, Colorado.

These same guidelines apply when using a slat wall fixture. One shelf up high for your vignette may be sufficient, but you can also have another at waist height to hold titles in book easels. Too many shelves cut down on the visibility of specific titles on display. Zig-zagged Plexiglas shelves that feature the spine of the item and part of the cover are also available. "J" rack holders can showcase the cover without extending too far into the traffic path. Smaller, single-item J racks offer more options for placement than long J rack shelves.

A variety of slat wall accessories are the right tools for the job. Schlessman Family Branch, Denver Public Library, Colorado.

Sampling of slat wall accessories. Courtesy Demco, Inc.

Considerations in Choosing a Fixture

When choosing a fixture, there are some key questions you need to ask yourself.

Is it sturdy and well made?

It is very important that your fixtures are safe, strong, and stable and that they won't topple over. Make sure they don't have sharp edges or stick out too far into your traffic path. These fixtures need to last through a lot of handling, so they should be made of durable materials, such as wood, Plexiglas, or metal. Cardboard might be cheap, but it isn't going to hold up under the weight of books and the handling of dozens of library customers. The cardboard dumps provided by publishers to promote a certain title may be exciting to have. However, after several months of use, they need to be retired because not only do they look bad, they are structurally unsound and likely to cause injury.

**A sturdy unit that offers many levels for materials is perfect for a children's display.
Jefferson County Public Library, Colorado.**

Is it flexible?

Use a fixture that has the potential to hold one or two types of materials. You want to be able to merchandise the entire collection from hardbound and paperback books to magazines and audiovisual titles. Your covers need to be showcased as well, so seek fixtures that offer face-out shelving options. Also, don't be lured in by architecturally intriguing fixtures. These usually end up taking the focus away from your display and the materials you want people to see, and they rarely give much display surface. Remember, your materials also need to be accessible, so avoid a fixture that puts your merchandise too low or too high.

**This piece serves double duty as seating and merchandising space.
Jefferson County Public Library, Colorado.**

Is it mobile?

Fixtures with relocating possibilities give you even more merchandising options. You don't want to move your fixtures around every week, because this confuses your customer, but mobility does give you some play with regard to the future. If you see that your designated display area needs to change because of design changes at your location, having fixtures on castors makes this transition simpler. If you do use these types of fixtures, make sure the wheels lock as a safety feature for your staff and customers.

A fixture on wheels offers options for relocating. Jefferson County Public Library and Bear Valley Branch, Denver Public Library, Colorado.

Fixture Vendors

Buying your fixtures need not be difficult. There are plenty of options just waiting to be shipped to your location from these library and retail vendors:

www.Demco.com

www.Brodart.com

www.thelibrarystore.com

www.hubert.com

www.franklinfixtures.com

www.cleardisplays.com

www.waltermartin.com

If you have a healthy budget for a specialty fixture to fit nicely in a certain space, contact a local craftsman to build a unit specific for you. Also, be flexible in your approach. The Koebel Library (Arapahoe Library District, Colorado) wanted to assemble a power wall. By combining five premade units they already had into a unique pattern, they created just what they wanted. Amy Greenland, Information Services Coordinator at Koebel Library, tells the humorous story that her library has received numerous customer comments from patrons who think their new book selection is less than what it should be. "By doing so much face-out display, it's almost hard some days to keep the shelves stocked. Books check out quicker and can give the impression our shelves are low."[2]

Power wall. Koebel Branch, Arapahoe Library District, Colorado.

SIGNS

Sign holders can help protect and preserve your signs. Freestanding "T" sign holders work well with table and shelves, and slat wall sign holders are also available. The same applies here as with fixtures—and the simpler the better. An 8 1/2 x 11-inch sign, either vertical or horizontal, gives you a good, standard format. As a branding technique, use the same size sign for all of your displays. Again, library catalogs offer many varieties.

A variety of sign holders available from Demco, Inc. Courtesy Demco, Inc.

IMPROVISING FIXTURES

Service desks make great display areas. Schlessman Family Branch, Denver Public Library, Colorado.

Can't purchase specialty fixtures? Well never fear, we are all about improvising. A lot of librarians have to use what's readily available. The key to making do with what you have is to make it look intentional. Here are the bargain alternatives.

- Card tables offer a good-sized surface area and are mobile. Use a tablecloth to make it appear more professional.

- Book carts are mobile alternatives. Be sure however, that your cart isn't too small for the space and provides the visibility you seek. Cover it with a tablecloth or paper to give it a more colorful or polished look. Keep your items as visible as possible by pulling them to the edge of the shelves.

- Service desks and counters can be great display areas, as long as your display doesn't impede your ability to work.

- Study tables and carrels can be used to surprise your customers. Again, make sure the display doesn't impede the space's original purpose, and keep it neat and tidy.

- Architectural features such as windowsills, ledges, or the tops of low bookshelves can do the trick as well.

- Traditional shelving units are always available. Shift or weed to create room within your traditional shelves for merchandising and displays. Traditional shelving displays also offer a great way to fill empty space if your collection is small.

- In lieu of risers or cubes, try paint cans, popcorn buckets, wooden crates, or boxes covered in beautiful wrapping paper or maps.

- Visit the local thrift stores, stop at yard sales, and put out an all-staff APB seeking items for risers and fixtures. Remember, keep it tasteful, consistent with your existing interior decorations, and make sure it is in excellent condition.

Book carts work well as instant displays. Schlessman Family Branch, Denver Public Library, Colorado.

Display in study carrel. Saxton B. Little Free Library, Columbia, Connecticut.

When choosing from what you have on hand, the rules of display placement still apply. Keep your makeshift fixtures placed along your traffic path, and keep them visible from a distance. When using what's readily available in your library, you still need the accessories mentioned earlier. Of course, there are fixture and riser alternatives, but some spending is necessary. No matter what your budget, we recommend purchasing a few book easels, because they work on any flat surface and do a great deal for the appearance of your display.

A windowsill is a display space many of us already have.
Schlessman Family Branch, Denver Public Library, Colorado.

SHINING STARS

As mentioned earlier, your materials are your stars. Fixture designer Judith West says, "store fixtures need to be enticing enough to get the customer to cross the lease lines, but never more important than the products."[3] Let the fixtures be your supporting cast and the materials the items that steal the show.

FACE-OUT ASSIGNMENTS

- Assess your existing fixtures.
- Do you have enough fixtures?
- Do you have a budget for more fixtures?
- Do you have enough accessories to support your display fixtures?
- What alternative fixtures could you use?

NOTES

1. Chappell, Renee. "Getting a Fix on Fixtures." *Gourmet Retailer* (August 2002): 184–186.

2. Amy Greenland, e-mail to Jenny LaPerriere, August 30, 2007.

3. "Judith West's Fixtures Ensure That the Merchandise Is Always the Star: For Veteran Store Fixture Designer It's Not about Design for Design's Sake, but about Supporting the Brand and the Lifestyle." *Stores: The Bulletin of the N.R.D.G.A.* 85, no. 3 (2003): 64–66.

FURTHER READING

"Interview with Ron Godowski, of Gerrity's Supermarkets: Creating the Fixtures That Make Retail Store Operations Efficient and Profitable." *Progressive Grocer* 85, no. 2 (February 1, 2006): 95.

The Retail Environments Association, "What Are Store Fixtures?" http://www.nasfm.org/tools_indoverview.cfm (accessed July 6, 2007).

5

Anatomy of a Display

In the retail world, stores often hire a *merchandiser* or *visuals* person, who is responsible for either creating displays from the ground up or following a schematic or planogram that their corporate headquarters has sent.

Clothing planogram. Reproduced with permission from SmartDraw.com. http://www.smartdraw.com.

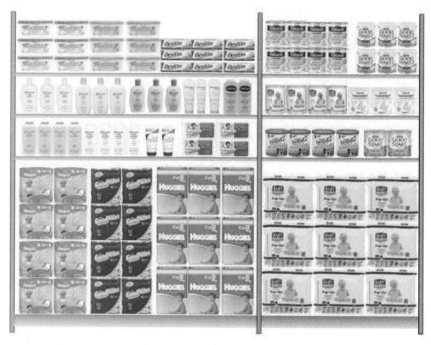

**Baby products planogram. Reproduced with permission from
SmartDraw.com. http://www.smartdraw.com.**

Having a schematic or planogram ensures a cohesive look to any display. Creating your own schematic is the first step to your dynamic display. To bring your vision to life, you will start with a theme, proceed to props, recognize the usefulness of color, and top it all off with signage. Let's take a closer look at the process.

IN THE BEGINNING

The best place to begin is with a theme. Themes can come from a variety of sources including, but not limited to:

- *Chase's Calendar of Events*
- Databases, such as *Reader's Advisor Online, NoveList,* and *Fiction Connection*
- Bibliographies and reading lists ("1950s Crime Novels" or "The Best Non-Fiction of 2008")

- Online listserves such as *Fiction_L, WebJunction,* or *PUBYAC* (check archives for themes and lists)

- Print readers' advisory guides such as the Genreflecting Advisory Series

- Current community, city, or state events

- Magazine and newspaper articles

- Library and trade publications ("Bestselling Cookbooks of the Year" or "Books Come to the Big Screen")

- Movies

- Staff

- Full areas in the collection

- Inspiration from retail displays

- Other libraries

- Interesting titles

Often themes just jump off the shelf at you. What area do you need to weed, but don't have time? What items are being requested most often? What is an upcoming holiday or event? Is there a community event you can tie in to? What time of year or season is it? Answering any of these questions can give you a theme.

Staff can be a wonderful resource. In your building, you have a variety of interests and knowledge. Just ask, and you'll be amazed at the opportunities so close to you.

HAPPY HOLIDAYS

Holidays are by far the easiest themed display to do. If you are doing a holiday themed display, it should be up 30 to 60 days before the holiday. Retail stores have their Christmas merchandise out as early as October.

By having the holiday items out early, you increase the number of times they will circulate before the holiday arrives. If you still have Easter books at Easter, your display didn't do its job.

Once the holiday has passed, change your display and promote the next one. Your Valentine's Day items should be off display on February 15. Create a calendar that will show when your holiday displays will go up and how long they will run.

A "Witches in Fiction" display shows that Halloween isn't just for kids. Schlessman Family Branch, Denver Public Library, Colorado.

Easter is another holiday that offers more than just children's titles. Schlessman Family Branch, Denver Public Library, Colorado.

A chart is particularly handy and a great visual tool. However, with any dated material you must remember to update it once a year to reflect the new dates.

2007 Displays National Holidays

JAN	FEB	MAR	APR	MAY	JUN	JUL	AUG	SEP	OCT	NOV	DEC

MLK's BDAY
12/20 – 1/21

Cinco de Mayo
4/1-5/5

4th of July
6/15 – 7/4

Hispanic Heritage Month
9/1-9/30

Veteran's Day
10/20 – 11/11

Black History Month
2/1-2/28

Halloween
9/15 – 10/31

Valentine's Day
1/15-2/14

Women's History Month
3/1-3/31

Flag Day
6/1-6/14

Family History Month
10/1 – 10/31

President's Day
1/15-2/18

Mother's Day
5/1-5/10

Thanksgiving
10/1 – 11/22

Spring Begins
3/1-3/20

Father's Day
6/1-6/15

Patriot Day
9/1-9/11

New Year's
12/1-1/1

Chinese New Year
1/20 – 2/7

A holiday chart.

MAIN EVENTS

The rule about timeliness also applies to national holidays such as Election Day or community events such as museum exhibits. You want to create interest and provide information before the actual date arrives. Stay apprised of upcoming museum exhibits or community events for theme ideas through their websites or mailing lists.

Let other community organizations know what you are doing, and chances are you will get great props and promotional material from them. One call to the local roller derby team for "National Roller Skating Month" (October) yielded posters, buttons, a T-shirt, and free tickets for a drawing. Think of those non-holiday calendar dates as well. Early March is a perfect time to set up a tax display featuring the newest tax-aid titles. Early August is ripe for back-to-school titles and tie-ins. Think of displays as an extension of your community outreach and programming.

An Election Day display needs to be up well before November. Schlessman Family Branch, Denver Public Library, Colorado.

A mummy display coordinated with a museum exhibit. Schlessman Family Branch, Denver Public Library, Colorado.

Chinese New Year is an often overlooked February event. Schlessman Family Branch, Denver Public Library, Colorado.

VIGNETTES

Vignettes offer a brief visual description of the featured items, where you can see your items in action. Visit your local interior decorating store and see how they merchandise products in situ. They use vignettes such as creating place settings on a dining room table complete with dishes, flatware, linens, candles, vases, and a centerpiece, or a bed made up in linens with pillows and throws.

**A tablescape conveys the "big picture" to a customer.
The Complete Gourmet, Centennial, Colorado.**

In retail, vignettes are designed to show the customer how the merchandise will look in use. For libraries, vignettes provide picture recognition of your display theme, since the actual book titles can't be read from far away. Vignettes are where you can get crafty. Need a dish of ice cream? Whip one up with some fabric, stuffing, and an ice cream bowl. Need a fingerprint card and mug shot? Enlist a willing staff member to help with the honors. However, keep in mind again the difference between homemade and handmade. Always keep your display professional looking. The vignette should instantly convey the theme to the customer. If you can't figure out what the topic is from your vignette, then you need to rethink it.

**This Spring Cleaning vignette would be understood even without the sign.
Schlessman Family Branch, Denver Public Library, Colorado.**

Vignettes should only be 10 percent of your entire display space, so don't over clutter your display with lots of little doodads and signs. Remember we want to "sell" the library materials, not the tchotchkes. A standard library vignette serves as a backdrop, with one to three props and a sign. If you are using a shelving unit, then your vignette should be on the top shelf. On a table, the vignette should be at the highest point.

GOTTA GIVE PROPS

Props are the jewelry of your display. You never wear every necklace you own, and the same is true with props. Have you ever seen something in a store you wanted only to find out that it wasn't for sale? This is why your props need to be accents that do not detract from the circulating titles. The beauty of props is that they can be found anywhere. Ask staff members to search through their homes and bring in items before throwing them away. Check yard sales and secondhand stores. Local craft stores also have fun and useful decorative accents. When choosing props, make sure they are multipurpose. Come up with at least two display themes before purchasing a prop.

Variations on a theme shows the same vignette in different ways.
Schlessman Family Branch, Denver Public Library, Colorado.

The same prop used in different displays. Denver Public Library, Colorado.

Start your prop closet with some seasonal and holiday items. A miniature artificial pine tree can be used as a Christmas tree, but undecorated it can also accent a Nevada Barr, outdoor mystery-style display, or a bear display. Put some eggs in a basket for Easter and National Preparedness Month (September). A rubber chicken fits the bill for an April Fool's Day display on jokes or humorous fiction. It gets easier once you get those creative juices going.

Besides being multipurpose, props need to be inexpensive. Our rule of thumb is "only use what you're willing to lose" so leave grandma's antique vase at home. Some props can be glued to a cardboard base or hung up high to deter theft, but there are no guarantees. Keep your props in proportion to your fixture. Props should be no more than 10 percent of your display. Another prop rule is that the larger the prop, the fewer you use.

A rodeo display needs few props, due to the size of the saddle used. Schlessman Family Branch, Denver Public Library, Colorado.

Props ideas can also come from the Dewey classifications.

000–199 Computer mouse and disks

200–299 Religious icons

300–399 School supplies, green plastic army men

400–499 Maps, writing implements

500–599 Animals, beakers, rulers

600–699 Cooking utensils, flowers, tools, baby bottle, toy cars

700–799 Craft items, decorating samples, art supplies, sporting equipment

800–899 Writing implements, plaster bust

900–999 Maps, globes, flags

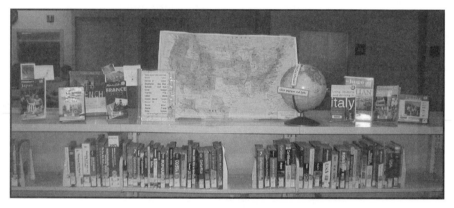

A globe and map make perfect travel props. Ross-Cherry Creek Branch, Denver Public Library, Colorado.

Beginning Prop Inventory

- Vases and containers such as urns
- Silk flowers, small trees
- Small rocks or stones to fill in vases
- Suitcase or briefcase
- Fake foods
- Picture frames
- Tablecloths and fabrics

- Kitchen utensils
- Globe
- Holiday accents (menorah, basket, heart, flag)
- Art supplies (brush, canvas, paint)
- Toys (bucket, car, board game)
- Papers (wrapping, maps)

Prop Rules

- Props should be no more than 10 percent of your display.
- The larger the props, the fewer props in the display.
- If in doubt, leave it out.
- Less is more.
- Props shouldn't be valuable or irreplaceable.

Inexpensive toy soldiers are expendable props. Schlessman Family Branch, Denver Public Library, Colorado.

Last Prop Rule

A store excites us because of its newness. You are the potential new owner of the merchandise. Even in antique and secondhand stores, the merchandise is cleaned, polished, and fixed, ready for its new owner. When using props, keep in mind that they must be in good condition. Anything broken, torn, worn out, or otherwise damaged just doesn't look appealing and conveys to the customer that perhaps the featured library materials aren't that special either. Consider your props disposable. If they break, toss them out. You want your props to shine alongside the attractive collection you are promoting.

Valuable props in a diorama on traditional shelving also act as a classification sign for this children's section. Arapahoe Library District, Colorado.

COVER-UPS

Fabric or paper can add another dimension to your display. Whether to soften the effect or set the tone, these items can be wrapped around a piece of foam board for a vignette backdrop or laid flat as a tablecloth. When using a book cart or card table, fabric and paper can add a bit of pizzazz and cover up the base item that might not be so new. Again, you need whatever you use to be neat and tidy, so either hem the fabric or make sure the edges aren't frayed. Merchandising consultant Renee Chappell says that one of the biggest display mistakes is "using wrinkled and frayed fabrics."[1]

These also need to serve more than one display, so try for solids and textures and avoid overly specific or novelty prints.

Tablecloth used two ways. Schlessman Family Branch, Denver Public Library, Colorado.

- Fabric should have hemmed edges, be wrinkle free, and clean. Basic solid, primary colors can be used repeatedly. Metallics, velvet, and taffeta can also come in handy. Shop your local fabric store's bargain bin for these more expensive fabrics.

- Maps from travel brochures, weeded travel books, or old topography maps work well with any kind of travel display. If the map is not in pristine condition after the display is over, just recycle it and get a newer map for your next display.

- Wrapping paper is a great inexpensive alternative and comes in a variety of patterns, colors, and textures. As with maps, recycle the paper if it shows wear and tear after the display.

- Tablecloths can be layered for a unique look. Try having a patterned cloth under a solid one to give your materials an uncluttered background.

A paper background serves as the sign for this display and makes the materials "pop." Schlessman Family Branch, Denver Public Library, Colorado.

COLOR

Color can make or break a display. Is the use of color in your display for accent or tone, or is it the display? Will it carry the display or only assist? Artists enlist the power of color when creating cover art, so chances are that similarly themed titles will be the same color. Books having anything to do with Ireland tend to be green. Chick lit leans toward perky pinks, purples, and yellows. True crime titles often make a statement with red and black. Your use of color can be the very thing that pulls customers to your display, much like what pulls customers to the cover of an item.

"When someone enters a new environment they function at a fourth grade level no matter what their actual education level is and color can give them direction or tell them the theme,"[2] says Renee Chappell, merchandising consultant. Fixture designer Judith West knows the importance of color: "color is the universal language ... customers feel a certain warmth and allure when they see colors."[3] Think of all the possibilities you can bring with the use of color.

So, how can you use color?

- Color as accent: A simple red rose is all that is needed for a romance fiction display.

- Color as tone: A backdrop of red fabric, a knife with red "blood," and a "bloody" footprint scream that they are working for a true crime display.

- Color as a display: All books with red covers for a "Have you REaD This?" February display.

Specific colors can evoke moods and convey topics. Here are some ideas:

- Red—heat, passion, danger, love, Valentine's Day

- Orange—warmth, autumn, Halloween, hunger

- Yellow—caution, summer, joy

- Green—nature, envy, spring, Ireland

- Blue—water, calming, depression, Chanukah

- Violet—exotic, royal, shyness

- Black—mystery, elegance, night

- White—pure, sterile, winter

- Brown—earth, nature

AND THE SIGN SAYS

Signage can be an integral part of your display, and also convey your brand. It can at once tell you the theme by being informative, or it can be entertaining by adding a humorous touch. The retail world has always embraced the power of signage. In an article for the banking industry, Tom Chekel lists thirteen basic guidelines for signs including uniformity, reinforcing brand image, and the less-is-more concept.[4] You can spread your creative talents with signage. However, as with all the other aspects of a display, the signage should be clear and professional. A sign should not be handwritten unless this could be an integral part of the display such as "epistolary fiction" or "calligraphy."

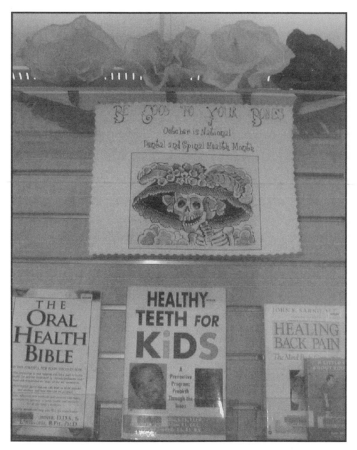

Signs need to be part of your display and not an afterthought. Schlessman Family Branch, Denver Public Library, Colorado.

Follow this sign etiquette when producing the signage in your display:

- Keep it simple and short.
- If a lot of text is needed, consider leaving out props.
- Use crisp, bold, high-contrast letters.
- Use a mix of upper- and lowercase fonts—this will be easier to read than all capital letters. Also avoid overly ornate script fonts.
- Fill the page symmetrically.
- What is the sign adding to your display?
- Does the sign distract?
- Choose a complementary paper color for your display. If in doubt, use white.
- Secure the sign in a proper holder.

A sign can also serve as the vignette. Schlessman Family Branch, Denver Public Library, Colorado.

FILL 'ER UP

Once it is fully stocked, your display is ready to make its debut. You need enough titles to keep your display full for its run. A display isn't much to look at if it's only got a few titles, but you also don't want to empty your shelves. Don't use a hot, new best seller for a display, because that title is already in your new titles location and it will sell itself. Also don't use a title that has a lot of holds on it. You want to promote a title, not keep it away from the customer. Such is the paradox of displays. You need to find a balance. The key is to use titles from your collection that have appeal but might otherwise go unnoticed.

Decide on a system for gathering display titles. Some libraries are able to request titles from other locations, but others are discouraged from doing this. If you can only use items from your own library, then keep your displays in proportion to your collection. If you are able to request materials from other branches, don't request titles that will be missed there. In early fall everyone is looking for titles on apples, pilgrims, Halloween, and leaves. These items will be popular at their home location, too. If you're working with a popular subject, just pull materials from your own collection. Get creative and pull from other areas—for a fall theme, consider adding horror fiction, costume sewing, party decorating, or crock pot cooking.

Before stocking your display, decide whether you want to check out titles to a display library card or change the location status in the catalog. You might find that your displays move so fast and are so numerous that you cannot keep up with checking out all of the titles or changing their status. However, you do want to make sure you can find them when they are needed. If you do not change the status of display copies, then you need to inform your staff of your display themes to assist them with title location. Create a display "key" and post it in visible locations to help the staff with restocking and fluffing.

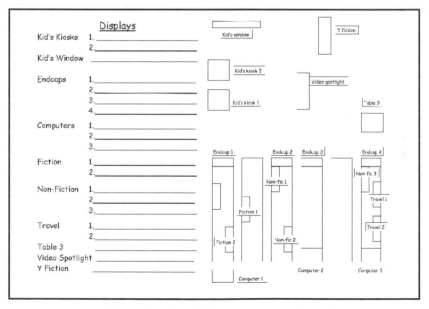

A display location list keeps everyone informed.

Stocking and Fluffing

Imagine cruising the aisle of your local supermarket. The end caps are nicely stocked with the featured items of the week. They look appealing. Rows and rows of chips in perfect lines look charming and appeal to your hunger or aesthetics. If the end cap only had one or two bags of chips haphazardly displayed, it wouldn't look nearly as attractive. The same goes for your library displays.

Customers are always drawn to a full and attractive retail display. Denver Zoo, Colorado. Courtesy of K.M. Concessions.

Displays need to be stocked and fluffed constantly. *Stocked* means that there are ample items for customers to choose from. *Fluffed* means that items are all faced forward, sitting straight in their stands, and eagerly awaiting customers. While you want your display full, you don't want it stuffed. You want your customer to be able to see each item. Titles can be staggered, but make sure all covers are visible and accessible. Stocking and fluffing a display needs to happen on a continual basis throughout the day, every day—especially on weekends and when your library is busy. If your display empties out quickly, then congratulations. You did a great job, but be ready to stock it again. If your theme doesn't have an abundance of titles to begin with, then be prepared to take down your display and put up another one in its place. If your display doesn't move, don't take it personally or get your feelings hurt. Move on quickly. It may work in another place or time.

KEEP IT CLEAN AND SAFE

Make sure what you include in your display is clean, attractive, and safe. Don't display items with dirty or torn covers. Avoid items with plain library bindings. (We go into more detail about item attractiveness in Chapter 6, "Housekeeping.") It is fine to display oversized items, but make sure they are not balanced precariously where they could fall on someone.

GO WITH THE FLOW

Item placement within your display plays a very important part in its success. Each display has a flow in which the customer's eye will travel when viewing it. One retail technique is to arrange your items in a pyramid shape with smaller items on the ends and the larger ones in the middle. When seen straight on, the pyramid is a pleasing shape, and it draws the eye along to each item.

Another arrangement is the stair step. This works well when the items are viewed from an angle to ensure that all covers are seen. If your customer is approaching the display from the side, have smaller titles or stacks first, leading to larger ones.

The pyramid layout is a common retail technique.

Stair-stepped stacks make every cover visible. Schlessman Family Branch, Denver Public Library, Colorado.

It really can be love at first sight with a display and a customer. You want your customers to see your display and what it has to offer. Their gaze will pick up on one thing, be it the color or a prop or the sign. Then they will take in all the aspects, including what you are really selling: the library materials.

FAIT ACCOMPLI

You now have all the tools to create a display. Once you have your display assembled, step back and make sure that everything is visible and facing the customer. Do any necessary tweaking to ensure your sign and all of your covers are seen. The important thing is to have fun with your displays. Displays are your opportunities to showcase your creativity and to make your library more inviting. Displays are tools to make your job easier because your collection is doing the work for you. Find that inner Martha Stewart and go for it.

FACE-OUT ASSIGNMENTS

- Pick a theme.
- Choose colors.
- Gather props.
- Make signage.
- Assemble your display.
- Check signage and props. Too much? Too little?
- Are items facing in a direction so that the customer will see them?
- What is your plan to stock and fluff the display?

NOTES

1. Renee Chappelle (Renee Chappelle & Associates), interviewed by Jenny LaPerriere and Trish Christiansen, March 22, 2007.
2. Ibid.
3. West, Judith. "Judith West's Fixtures Ensure That the Merchandise Is Always the Star." *Stores* 85 (March 2003): 64–66.
4. Chekel, Tom. "Good Sign." *ABA Bank Marketing* 33 (June 2001): 36.
5. Ibid.

FURTHER READING

Cahan, Linda. "Thanks for Thanksgiving." *Gifts & Decorative Accessories* 102, no. 9 (September 2001): 26–28.

Cahan, Linda. "The 'Wow' Factor: The Power of Good Display Merchandisers and Props Will Pay for Themselves in Short Order." *Gifts & Decorative Accessories* 106, no. 2 (February 2005): 18.

Camilletti, Tony. "Signage & Graphics Trends." *Display & Design Ideas* 19, no. 9 (September 2007): 96.

Carleton, Jesse. "A Giant Reborn: Keim Lumber Expands into the 21st Century with a Stunning New Look." *Hardware Retailing* 192, no. 5 (May 2007): 122–126.

Chappell, Renee. "Dramatic Presentation." *Gourmet Retailer* 24, no.10 (October 2003): 68–70.

Chappell, Renee. "A Rainbow of Options." *Gourmet Retailer* 23, no.1 (October 2002): 61–63.

Geary, Donna. "Signing: Putting Silent Communications to Work." *Pet Commerce* 1, no. 5 (June/July 1999): 15–20.

Gorman, Greg. *Visual Merchandising and Store Design Workbook: Merchandising, Fixturing and Lighting Create Visual Excitement for Retail Stores*. Ohio: ST Publications, 1998. 111p. $24.95. ISBN 0944094201.

Pearl, Nancy. *Book Crush for Kids and Teens: Recommended Reading for Every Mood, Moment, and Interest*. Seattle: Sasquatch Books, 2007. 288p. $16.95. ISBN 1570615004.

Pearl, Nancy. *Book Lust: Recommended Reading for Every Mood, Moment, and Reason*. Seattle: Sasquatch Books, 2003. 287p. $16.95. ISBN 1570613818.

Pegler, Martin M. *Store Presentation & Design No. 2: Branding a Store*. New York: Visual Reference Publications, 2007. 174 p. $40.00. ISBN 1584711094.

Roberts, Jo. "Signs of Improvement." *In-Store* (April 2007): 25–27.

Saxton, Lisa. "Creative Merchandising Is Called Key to Profits." *Supermarket News* 42, no. 12 (March 23, 1992): 36.

Seidler, Lori. "If You Build It, They Will Party: Seasonal Displays Provide Extra Lift for Store Sales, So How Can Retailers Keep the Party Going All Year?" *Private Label Buyer* 22, no. 3 (March 2008): 48.

Valentine, Matthew. "Please Sign Here." *In-Store* (March 2004): 25–27.

6

Housekeeping

   Product quality and attractiveness is key for successful merchandising. Every morning before opening and every evening after closing, personnel in retail stores straighten, refill, and clean their stores. A clean store is much more appealing to the customer than one with stained carpet and dusty shelves. The *2005 Store Atmospheric Study* reveals that the most fundamental element of the shopping environment is cleanliness.[1] The same philosophy applies to the merchandise itself. No one wants to buy merchandise that looks dirty and used. In fact, some customers have told us that they will buy a new book before checking one out of the library because of sanitary issues. Besides, it's more exciting to be the first one to see and touch new merchandise. Even though your goal may be to get a title into as many hands as possible, your library is not a yard sale. Customers will always pick a clean, newer copy over one that is falling apart. With a little extra care and maintenance, you can ensure a long, healthy life for your collection.

These tidy cases make the product more appealing. Carnival Supermarket, Texas. Courtesy api(+).

THINNING THE HERDS

A well-weeded collection is a well-circulating collection. This is important because we want to ensure our materials are used, useful, and usable. There are many benefits to continuous weeding:

- You save space.

- You save time for your staff and customers.

- You make your collection more appealing and valuable.

- You enhance your library's reputation and image for having current information.

- You have a continuous check on your collection's condition, including any strengths or weaknesses.

All libraries have different weeding procedures, but if you stay on top of it, you can ensure a viable collection. If a book has become so worn out that it cannot be repaired without looking shabby, then it needs to be retired. If it is a title you need in your collection, order a replacement copy. If an item is outdated or hasn't circulated in years, then consider weeding it.

Displays are a great opportunity to give otherwise forgotten titles a second lease on life, yet if the information inside is no longer accurate, it needs to go. This will free up space on your shelves for newer, more pertinent editions.

SHIFT IT

If you can't fit a bookend on the shelf, then it is time to weed or shift. Having at least six to twelve inches of space on your shelves gives breathing room to your ever-changing collection and allows customers to access materials more easily. Shelvers or pages can shift on a continual basis when reshelving titles. When shifting titles up or down a shelf, try not to insert a break in the same classification number, author, or title. Think of the crescent shape and keep the majority of titles within the middle shelves. When an area gets too full, it can also be an indication that a display needs to be done.

Adequate space on shelves for shifting and face outs.
Schlessman Family Branch, Denver Public Library, Colorado.

LOOKS LIKE NEW

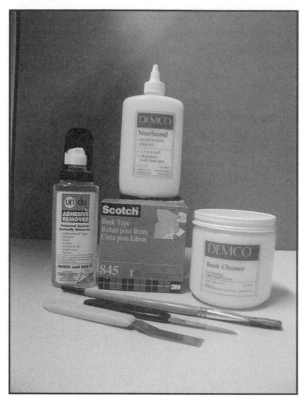

A supply of cleaning products will keep your collection looking its best.

When one thinks of a library, it might conjure up images of old dusty tomes and musty smells. Although it is a fact of library life that over time, items become dirty and cases broken, you don't want your customers to feel like archaeologists discovering the lost collection of Alexandria. Cleaning your collection is necessary for sanitary reasons, as well as for increasing a title's appeal. Invest in book cleaner, spare cases, and dust jacket covers. Replace any labels that peel off or yellow. The same thing goes for your shelves and fixtures themselves. Dust and cobwebs do not add importance to your collection. Make sure your shelves and books get dusted and cleaned regularly. In retail, salespeople are taught to handle each item like it costs a million dollars, because customers desire items they perceive to be valuable and will generally take better care of them.

Changing labels and book jackets make an enormous difference in the appearance of your materials. Central Branch, Denver Public Library.

FLUFF IT UP

Even though an empty shelf is a sign of success, no one wants to shop from a display that looks like it's already been picked through. Every customer deserves to see a brand-new display, so always keep your shelves full. How appealing is only one bag of potato chips on a grocery store end cap? Customers want to see full displays. It conveys to them that what they are looking at or shopping for is so important that we carry lots of it. For your staff this means that everyone needs to be involved in "fluffing" your collection. Fluffing is a retail term meaning refilling and pumping up. Replacing items in your displays and facing out titles in your shelves gives them a fresh new feeling all throughout the day.

Even though "mess = success," displays always need to look brand new.
Schlessman Family Branch, Denver Public Library, Colorado.

BACK STOCK

Keep a back stock of books for staff to easily refill your displays. Remember, having to refill a display many times shows that your collection is moving. On the same note, you need to have enough products to fill your display area. Don't pick a theme so specific that you only have a few books to choose from. Keep this in mind when deciding on your display fixtures as well. You don't want a large multitiered table if you are only able to have a few books on display at a time.

A brand new display begins on a large table to accommodate the many copies. Schlessman Family Branch, Denver Public Library, Colorado.

The same display moved to a smaller space after items have been checked out. Schlessman Family Branch, Denver Public Library, Colorado.

STORAGE

Storage is another important tool for successful display maintenance. Start with an area that you can use as storage for your shelves, Plexiglas accessories, and props. A filing cabinet or cupboard for signs, bookmarks, theme ideas, and title lists is also useful. Create a map showing where your displays are to assist in finding titles for the customer. Print out a new map every month and keep it at any service desk for your staff to see. Designate a display area, and, like any good first aid kit, keep it stocked with the supplies you need.

In a binder or filing cabinet, keep:

- Map of display locations

- Fixture schematics

- Ideas for themes and title lists

- List of previous displays and notes on their success

- Calendar of display rotation

On a shelf or in a closet, put:

• Props sorted by category in clear containers

• Label containers

• Enough containers so as not to crush or fold items

• Containers with lids to elude dust

• Sign holders and other fixture accessories

Prop storage. Schlessman Family Branch, Denver Public Library, Colorado.

LIFE SPAN OF A DISPLAY

Another decision you need to make is how long your displays will stay up. Our experience shows that a month is sufficient for a well-designed display. Do you want to do all of your displays at once or spread them throughout the month? A rotation system in which a different display is set up each week can ease the creative burden of trying to do everything at once. Decide the chronological order of your display fixture setups and create a calendar to reflect this. Planning out on a calendar will keep everyone apprised and your merchandisers prepared.

Another option is to set all of your displays once a month. Around mid-month, decide on the themes, make signs, and collect props and titles for the upcoming month. Before opening, all of the displays are switched out for a fresh new look at the start of each month. Customers may even learn your schedule for setup and look forward to each new display.

LET IT GO

Don't get your feelings hurt if a display doesn't take off. Take it down and move on. Maybe it wasn't the right time or location. You can always try it again later. Generally, displays have a two- to four-week shelf life. They take a week to get noticed, then fly for two weeks, and finally slow down in the last week. You may find a display does well for two weeks then peters out. Don't put it on life support and ignore the fact that nothing is moving. Take it down and put another display in its place.

FACE-OUT ASSIGNMENTS

- Create a weeding schedule and make assignments.
- Who is responsible for cleaning parts of the collection?
- Make a dusting schedule and check it on a continual basis.
- Make a display schedule for the upcoming year.
- Organize your props.
- Train staff to "fluff" and "face out" displays and shelves.

NOTE

1. Wilson, Marrianne. "Atmospheric Key to Well-Being." *Chain Store Age* 81, no. 10 (October 2005): 94.

7

Enlisting and Educating Staff

YES, YOU!

Merchandising can be extremely fun and rewarding. Once the merchandising bug hits, you see possibilities everywhere. Excitement builds and a passionate flood of merchandising and creativity is unleashed on your collection. Of course, when it comes to merchandising, the biggest factor for success is the staff, and you will have the most positive results with everyone on board. Utilize everyone's strengths, and let your staff participate at the level they are most comfortable. Some of your staff will be anxious to flex their creative muscle. Some staff are more of the idea types, and not as strong with the implementation. Merchandising doesn't have to be a time-consuming task. Initially, it takes some work to determine your display areas, tidy up your general collection, and accumulate some props and bibliographies. Once you get going, you will be amazed at how easy it becomes. The key is to remain organized and not to do more than you can handle. Remember, you want this to be fun as well.

Keep your staff members involved at every step by asking for their input and ideas and explaining your process. You want the entire staff to be passionate about connecting the customers and the collection in more seamless and exciting ways. The benefits are high when everyone has a sense of ownership.

WANTED

A whole new mind-set in library personnel is needed when it comes to merchandising. "Merchandising" is seldom part of a library school curriculum, and it is often just left up to the most creative person on the staff. A text about store displays puts it best:

> visual merchandising is both an art and a science, combining elements of subjective creativity and objective merchandising standards.[1]

As noted in Chapter 1, those doing the merchandising need to "get it." Although you want everyone on your staff to be involved and knowledgeable, you can't afford to have your collection presentation standards (CPS) and displays look sloppy, poorly planned and executed, or not well maintained. A current retail text bluntly spells it out:

> The simple truth is that the last people to handle the merchandise before the customers make an evaluation are the lowest paid on the staff. These employees are rarely trusted with making independent judgments on presentation policy, mainly because there is no corporate guideline for aesthetics. And yet these same employees are exactly the people who need exposure to aesthetic principles the most. They need to consider themselves as professionals—as contributing associates to forming and maintaining policy—especially on the sales floor.[2]

This could have been expressively written for the library community. Even in the retail world, finding and training staff can be a challenge, but it is a critical element of your success.

Those that have worked in retail settings generally understand and know the concepts. When posting for any position, place "retail experience helpful" in the ad. All library staff members will be walking the floor at some point and need to know what looks right and what needs fluffing. The person or persons who will specifically be doing the majority of the merchandising needs to have these qualities:

- Creative

- Artistic

- Be willing to think outside the box

- Have physical endurance to stand on ladders, bend low, lift heavy items

- Have worked in retail or understand retail concepts through astute shopping
- Be open to suggestions and ideas
- Always be on the lookout for new ideas when in the retail world
- Be able to share resources among other libraries
- Solicit ideas from other libraries and colleagues

YOU'RE HIRED

The merchandiser(s) should be fully on board with the concept. While you want all of your staff involved, merchandising works best if one or two staff members are designated as your main merchandisers. They will be responsible for CPS quality assurance and creating and maintaining displays. That said, involving the entire staff at some level ensures that everyone is knowledgeable about the concept. If you are unable to employ someone as sole merchandiser, then look for staff members who are creative but also able to prioritize their duties. By staying organized, your merchandisers will be able to do a bit here and there as time permits.

All staff members can fluff and restock a display as they walk by it. All staff members can keep the library attractive. Your staff represents a plethora of interests, talents, and knowledge. They can be an artistic gold mine and an endless source of display ideas. However, make it clear the merchandising direction you are going and what you expect.

TRAINING

All staff need training in CPS and your own merchandising standards. Having a clear document with photographs of exactly what you want will leave little room for error. Those who will actually be doing the merchandising on a continual basis will need hands-on instruction. Standards apply just as they do with any other part of the job. Materials have to be shelved according to the classification system, and they need to be presented according to CPS.

Rework all or part of your collection to reflect CPS and your standards. Set guidelines as to how it is maintained and by whom. The training stage is when you can impress upon the staff your excitement and expectations for the attractiveness of the collection. Training doesn't happen just once. Keep in motion ongoing workshops, field trips, and idea sharing. Inspiration can come from anywhere, and you and your staff need to be sponges ready to absorb.

Visual merchandising is often part of the curriculum at local colleges and universities in schools of art and design. Make contacts with these institutions to build partnerships for continuing education. The National Association for Retail Marketing (www.narms.com/training) has an online training manual and test that you could incorporate into your training. Also, many local retailers and national chains would be more than happy to share their expertise with a public institution. We're "not for profit" and can only take their ideas so far; usually we are not seen as competitors.

DUTIES

Visit your local grocery store early in the morning and you will see them stocking the shelves and facing out the items. Likewise, your merchandiser should walk the floor before the library is open to check the following CPS and display structures:

- Crescent shape

- Items fronted

- Items faced out

- What areas need to be dusted, cleaned, picked up, and moved back to order?

- What areas need to be weeded?

- Fill and fluff displays

- Change or rotate displays

FAQs

We often receive questions after we give our merchandising presentation. The following FAQs and answers can further assist you with the training process. They might also give you backup and justification for your new venture.

"This makes us look like a bookstore and takes away from our purpose."
Is there anything wrong with looking like a bookstore? The goal in any library is to help customers locate items they need or didn't know they wanted. CPS and displays make this possible and easier.

"I'm a librarian, not a salesperson."

Au contraire. Aren't we "selling" our collection? Don't the tax-payers deserve to know how you have spent their money? Bringing forth the collection with consistent CPS and dynamic displays will ensure that collection is discovered, used, and appreciated.

"I heard that merchandising is really for full-service libraries"

Merchandising is for any library—public, school, academic, special, and even noncirculating. Merchandising advertises and makes available what your collection has to offer.

"It makes it difficult for staff to find particular items for customers with displays everywhere."

The key to avoid difficulty in finding a displayed title is to keep informed and organized. Make sure all of your staff knows what and where your displays are. A "display" library card or an item status change in the catalog can be a finding aid as well as a visual schematic listing where displays are located. Avoid using highly requested titles.

"It's too hard to keep up with."

Don't overwhelm yourself. Start small, and create only as many displays as you can comfortably maintain. CPS will take some initial time to set up, but once in place, all of your staff can easily keep it up. You may find that your displays are so successful, you'll have to increase the number you have.

"What if I don't have multiple copies of items?"

Merchandising doesn't dictate what you put in your collection. You use what you have. Facing out single copies can easily do the trick.

"How can I sell this to my staff?"

Number one, it's fun. It is an endless outlet of creative juices. Yes, it is a new mind-set, but we must change with the times. Are we still using card catalogs?

"Who does the merchandising?"

It is up to you to set the guidelines, standards, and expectations. Then assemble the staff members who can do this. They need to be excited and motivated. Being artistic helps. Hire staff with retail experience and an eye for detail.

"I don't have the money to spend on this."

You can do this with little or no money. CPS requires no money. Displays can be done very inexpensively. You can create displays on your traditional shelving and on existing spaces such as public service desks, tables, and windowsills.

"Where do I get display fixtures?"

All the library supply vendors now carry a variety of display fixtures. If your administration is onboard and you have a healthy budget to work with, you can have customer fixtures tailor-made for your spaces. Just remember to consider how the pieces can be used in the future, and ensure that they are mobile. Also, research vendors that supply retail establishments. There are endless fixtures that would work well in library settings that you might also see at your local supermarkets. Here are some examples of retail sites:

www.hubert.com

www.displays2go.com

www.tridisplay.com

www.displaywarehouse.com

www.ddionlinedirectory.com

GO FOR IT!

When you start to merchandise, the rewards you see from your higher circulating collection and customer appreciation are on the horizon. It is fun, it is easy, and it is about time we sing the praises of the collections we have. Show them off. Offer them up. Be bold in your execution.

FACE-OUT ASSIGNMENTS

- Write a merchandising job description for your location.
- Hire a merchandiser or decide which staff member will assume the position.
- Take field trips with staff to stores and discuss likes and dislikes and what would work for your library.
- Be positive about the merchandising that will take place in your library.

• Have brainstorming sessions with staff and secure commitments for being fearless, flexible, and fun in the new venture together.

NOTES

1. Barr, Vilma, and Katherine Field. *Stores: Retail Display and Design* (p. 10). Glen Cove, NY: PBC International, 1997. 178p. $42.50. ISBN 0866365303.

2. Weishar, Joseph. *The Aesthetics of Merchandising Presentation.* Cincinnati, OH: ST Media Group International, 2005. 195p. $75. ISBN 0944094473.

FURTHER READING

Bayless, Maggie, "Display Building 101." *Gourmet Retailer* 27, no. 6 (June 2006): 54–55.

Dodd, Annmarie. "(Style) Help Wanted: A Guide to Hiring the Right Merchandiser for Your Shop." *Golf World* 59, no. 19 (December 16, 2005): 51.

"Further Education: The Big Leap ... Merchandiser: The Essential Weekly Guide for Those Who Fancy Making a Complete Career Change." *The Guardian* (London) October 21, 2003, p. 38.

8

How Are You Doing?

MEASUREMENTS

Whether merchandising and displays is a new way of doing business for your library or a test pilot, you'll need to measure your impact. You've got staff buy-in, you got fixtures and props, and you're merchandising and doing displays. So how are you doing? As detailed record keepers, librarians have two formats: circulation and anecdotal.

GOING UP

The retail world of course measures the effectiveness of its merchandising and displays with sales. Retailers want to make a profit, and they are constantly pulling out all the stops to get us to hand over our dollars. Did the window display draw more customers inside who, in turn, spent money? Did the newest doodad at the checkout counter sell quickly? Did customers not only purchase the latest sweater arrival, but also the jewelry and handbag displayed with it on the mannequin?

Libraries of course can measure circulation. We can break it down in any category we'd like. Did all of the new displays in the fiction area get checked out? Did the fiction circulation increase after the displays? Does the circulation drop if the displays are not filled? Librarians are great at analyzing figures and crunching numbers. Prepare a spreadsheet with your "before" and "after" circulation figures. Be sure to include how many displays or types of merchandising your are tracking.

Fiction	Jan-08	# displays	CPS	Feb-07	# displays	CPS	Mar-07	# displays	CPS
	3562	0	no	3912	1	yes	4123	3	yes
Audios	Jan-08	# displays	CPS	Feb-07	# displays	CPS	Mar-07	# displays	CPS
	419	0	no	590	1	yes	708	3	yes

Spreadsheets can track the success of your merchandising and displays.

The figure above is a sample to get you started. Think about these statistics to monitor as well.

- What is being cross-merchandised? Audios with print? Travel magazines with travel books?

- How many times a day do the displays need to be stocked and fluffed?

- Are items at point of checkout (POCO)?

- Did displays move from traditional shelving to specialized fixtures?

- How much time do the shelvers need to maintain CPS?

- How much time is spent planning and implanting displays?

COLLECTING STORIES

Anecdotal evidence is another great skill librarians have. We use "stories" and how-we-did-good tales to justify everything from programming to collection to building design. Verbal communication about merchandising and displays can come from anyone, anytime, anywhere.

- Ask customers point blank if the display helped them locate an item.

- Keep a notebook at all public service desks for staff to write down comments.

- Solicit feedback on your web site.

- Start a blog about your merchandising and displays.

- Record traffic patterns by observations. Are customers always stopping at the first display? Is the aisle with the new slat wall end cap busier?

Again, make a spreadsheet to keep track of the comments. A sample spreadsheet follows.

Comments	Jan-08 Displays=0/CPS no	Feb-08 Displays=3/CPS yes
Customers		
In person		All the new books are checked out. I love that display. Who did those displays? Very cute. Mommy look! Dinosaur books. I remember reading this series when I was a kid.
Comment cards		It was very easy for me to find the books I wanted. I didn't know the library also had such a big selection of travel dvds until you put them with the travel books. Thanks!
Online		The resume books were right there when I needed them. Thanks a lot! After my son saw the display on RATS he wants one of his own.
Staff		I had to restock the fiction display 3x today. I never have a whole cart of new books to shelve at once now. More trash found in the teen section since the displays.

Sample spreadsheet.

WHAT WORKS

It is important for you also to track what works well and what doesn't. However, give it some time and don't take down a display after two hours. Record your comments in a location where all staff can have access and add to it. Over time, merchandising and displays will become second nature, but it is always good to have a document, like the sample that follows, to refer back to for "lessons learned" and getting monetary support.

Jan-08

CPS   Need more book easels for fiction stacks
         Reminded shelvers pbks aren't good for face outs unless they are in
         an easel
         All multiple copies in juv fiction stacks went out first day
         Shelvers did CPS with audios and it has really moved

Displays Display on Chinese New Year went out fast. Replaced with National
         Pancake Week.
         Prop for Valentines can be used for Vampire Romance display next
         month
         Needed quick display for empty unit: "A little something to read"-
         books that were under about 6"

         2 branches asked for photos and props to do knitting display in May.

         Display on study carrel by water fountain got all wet. Moved carrel.

FURTHER READING

Echeandia, Lisbeth. "Keep It Simple—Make It Clear." *Confectioner* 91, no. 9 (December 2006): 36.

Genesy, Dave. "Take the Merchandising Test." *American Libraries* 37, no. 4 (April 2006): 511.

Porter, Robin. "Plan Well for Merchandising Success." *Food Management* 40, no. 5 (May 2005): 32.

Robison, Jennifer. "The Retail Doctor's Visual Merchandising Checklist." *Dealernews* 44, no. 2 (February 2008): 102.

9

Display in a Box

This concept is designed to facilitate displays between locations and offer quick ideas. You want to conserve resources and not reinvent the wheel each time. *Display in a Box* is literally what the name implies. Each box includes title lists, a sign, and props. Boxes can be transported to another location, unpacked, and set up. Then, voilà! You have a display! We haven't included extensive bibliographies because they can become outdated, and not every library has every title. Wonderful, updated lists can be found in Readers' Advisor Online (check the browse section for read-alikes, or use the quick list feature to create your own), NoveList, FictionConnection, and a variety of bibliographic resources such as the Genreflecting Advisory series, the Read On series, and What Do I Read Next series. We have included ideas for display themes, props, and suggested authors and genres to get you started. Not all props have to be used in each display, and be prepared for props to get damaged or lost. Signage should be simple and part of your branded look. Although signs are listed, in many cases the items on display and a simple prop will convey a theme without a sign. Always think about cross-merchandising your collection. When appropriate, include books, magazines, audio books, music, movies, and other formats you may carry in your display. Bookmarks that can accompany the display are a great "free gift with purchase." Displays are also a great place to advertise electronic resources you have by including bookmarks or promotional materials on the subject. Lastly, keep the displays well stocked and fluffed. Be ready to put up another display if it proves popular or be ready to move on if it isn't successful.

Armchair Traveler

Collection: Travel journals

Props: Diary, mug

Signage: "Adventures from the Couch"

Art in Literature

Collection: Art history or fiction about the creation of famous masterpieces

Props: Paintbrushes, small framed art

Signage: "Art in Fiction"

**Art in fiction. Schlessman Family Branch,
Denver Public Library, Colorado.**

Baby

Collection: Parenting books, baby names

Props: Baby bottle, diapers

Signage: "Oh Baby!"

Bees

Collection: Beekeeping, honey, fiction about bees

Props: Plastic bee and honey pot

Signage: "So Bee It," "All Abuzz"

**Beekeeping. Schlessman Family Branch,
Denver Public Library, Colorado.**

Biblical Lives

Collection: Biblical fiction

Props: Palm fronds, earthenware pots, and woven fabric

Signage: "Women in the Bible"

Biblical women. Schlessman Family Branch, Denver Public Library, Colorado.

Birds

Collection: Bird guides, bird watching

Props: Binoculars, bird

Signage: "Fine Feathered Friends"

Bon Voyage

Collection: Travel, travel magazines, travel DVDs, audio books, fiction, cookbooks, art/museum books, and audio books

Props: Suitcases used for risers or leave top open and place items inside for display, tickets, postcards, or maps

Signage: "Paris in the Springtime," "Arrivederci," "Adios," "Know Before You Go"

**New Orleans travel display. Schlessman Family Branch,
Denver Public Library, Colorado.**

Car Care

Collection: Car repair manuals, bookmarks about e-resources such as Auto Repair Manual

Props: Toy car

Signage: "Vroom, vroom"

Careers

Collection: Resume books, vocational guides, test books

Props: Briefcase, bookmarks advertising eResources you carry in this field

Signage: "When I Grow Up, I Want To Be…"

Chick Lit

Collection: Ideas at www.chicklitbooks.com

Props: *Chicklets* gum, yellow chicks, package of peeps

Signage: "Chick Lit" or "Not Tonight Dear, I'm Reading"

**ChickLit display. Schlessman Family Branch,
Denver Public Library, Colorado.**

Chicken Soup

Collection: Titles in the *"Chicken Soup for the Soul"* series
Props: Cans of Campbell's chicken soup
Signage: None

Classic TV

Collection: Books about classic TV shows and actors, TV series on DVD
Props: TV antenna
Signage: None

Collectibles

Collection: Price guides to collectibles and antiques
Props: Baseball trading cards, stamps, and vase
Signage: "Cash in the Attic" or "For What It's Worth"

Computers

Collection: Computer and Internet how-to books and a/v
Props: Computer mouse and keyboard
Signage: "Caught in the Web"

Culinary Memoirs

Collection: Nonfiction food-related memoirs
Props: Tablecloth, salt and pepper shakers, wine glass
Signage: "Culinary Memoirs" or "A Life in a Nutshell"

Dating

Collection: Nonfiction, fiction, audios
Props: Tube of lipstick, empty men's cologne bottle
Signage: "Don't Go Blindly" or "Find-A-Mate"

Diets

Collection: Nutrition and diet nonfiction

Props: Scale

Signage: "Healthy Living"

Dog Days of Summer

Collection: Fiction books and audios about dogs

Props: Dog toys

Signage: "Dog Days of Summer"

Enough Already

Collection: Fiction and nonfiction (print and audio) inspired by the *The DaVinci Code* by Dan Brown.

Props: Map of Paris and small Eiffel Tower

Signage: "Enough Already"

Environmental Fiction

Collection: Environmental fiction, serious and funny

Props: Recycling bin

Signage: "Green Reads"

Etiquette

Collection: Etiquette nonfiction

Props: Wood "P" and "Q"

Signage: "You Can't Say That"

Fairy Tales with a Twist

Collection: Adult and young adult fiction titles such as *Wicked: The Life and Times of the Wicked Witch of the West* by Gregory Maguire or *Beauty: A Retelling of the Story of the Beauty and the Beast* by Robin McKinley

Props: Witch hat

Signage: "Never Too Old for a Fairy Tale" or "Fairytales with a Twist"

Food for Thought

Collection: Titles such as *Fast Food Nation* by Eric Schlosser, *The Omni-vore's Dilemma* by Michael Pollan, *Don't Eat This Book* by Morgan Spurlock, *Cod* and *Salt* by Mark Kurlanksy, and *Supersize Me* DVD

Props: Empty food containers and wrappers, salt shaker

Signage: "Food for Thought" or "Food to Go"

Games

Collection: *Hoyle's Rules of Games* and game books

Props: Pack of cards and chess set (all glued down)

Signage: "Play On" or "The Game's Afoot"

Golf

Collection: Books and audio visuals about golf

Props: Golf club and square of AstroTurf with golf ball glued on

Signage: "Fore"

Golf display. Schlessman Family Branch, Denver Public Library, Colorado.

Grilling

Collection: Grilling cookbooks

Props: Chef's hat, barbecue tongs

Signage: "Patio Dadio"

Guitars

Collection: How-to guides to guitar playing, song books, scores for guitars

Props: Small guitar

Signage: "Don't Fret"

Happiness

Collection: Fiction and nonfiction that is happy or about happiness

Props: Plastic smiley face

Signage: "Happiness Is Just a Good Book Away"

Home Repair

Collection: Nonfiction home repair, electrical, plumbing, roofs, etc.

Props: Paintbrush, electrical switch

Signage: "Try This at Home"

Ice Cream

Collection: Ice cream making and history books

Props: Dish and spoon

Signs: "We All Scream for Ice Cream"

Ice Cream display. Schlessman Family Branch, Denver Public Library, Colorado.

The Immigrant Experience

Collection: Contemporary and historical fiction; biographies and memoirs
Props: Battered suitcase used as backdrop or riser, Statue of Liberty
Signage: "The Immigrant Experience"

Investing

Collection: Nonfiction investing, stocks, bonds, real estate
Props: Paper play money
Signage: "It's Only Money"

Jane Austen Inspiration

Collection: Books and films inspired by the works of Jane Austen
Props: Lace doilies, antique-looking items, flowers
Signage: "Jane Says …" or "Enough Already"

Pride and Prejudice inspired display. Schlessman Family Branch,
Denver Public Library, Colorado.

Jokes

Collection: Joke books and humor writings, funny fiction

Props: Rubber chicken

Signs: "A man walks into a library ..."

**Hysterical fiction display. Schlessman Family Branch,
Denver Public Library, Colorado.**

K

Collection: Books with "1000" in the title such as "1001 Books You Must
Read before You Die"

Props: Wooden "K"

Signs: "K"

Kosher Fiction

Collection: Fiction with Jewish themes or characters
Props: None
Signage: "OY Fiction"

Language

Collection: Learning a language print and audio-visual
Props: Country flags
Signs: "Speak to Me"

Librarians

Collection: Librarians in fiction
Props: The "Nancy Pearl" shushing librarian doll
Signage: "Librarians in Fiction"

**Librarians in Fiction display. Schlessman Family Branch,
Denver Public Library, Colorado.**

Literary Recreation

Collection: Puzzle, tangram, quiz books

Props: Rubix cube, question marks, puzzle pieces

Signage: "Upgrade Your Brain" or "I'm puzzled"

Literary Recreation display. Schlessman Family Branch, Denver Public Library, Colorado.

Mommy Memoirs

Collection: Nonfiction mothering memoirs, serious and funny

Props: Baby bottle, tube of lipstick

Signage: "Cry Until You Laugh"

Mountaineering

Collection: Memoirs of mountaineering, DVDs about mountaineering, technical climbing books

Props: String of karabiners

Signage: "Climb Every Mountain: Mountaineers and Their Stories" or "Because It's There"

Everest display. Schlessman Family Branch, Denver Public Library. Colorado.

Movies from Books—Awards

Collection: Fiction, nonfiction, audio books, soundtracks, scripts, and the movie

Props: Popcorn tubs as risers, sample "ballots" (www.oscar.com), trophy

Signage: "Read it before you see it" or "And the Winner Is ..."

Oscar display. Schlessman Family Branch, Denver Public Library, Colorado.

Murder on the Menu

Collection: Culinary mysteries such as Diane Mott Davidson, Joanne Fluke, Tamar Myers, and LouJane Temple

Props: Checkered tablecloth, wooden spoon, bottle with poison symbol or dagger

Signage: "Murder on the Menu," or "Taste for Murder"

Murder on the Menu display. Schlessman Family Branch,
Denver Public Library, Colorado.

Music Inspired by Books

Collection: Ideas at www.siblproject.org/famous.html; include the book and the CD.

Props: Sheet music, concert tickets, instruments

Signage: "Music Inspired by Books" or "Melody of the Written Word"

National Craft Month

Collection: Craft books

Props: Craft supplies

Signage: "Get Crafty" or "March Is National Craft Month"

National Craft Month. Schlessman Family Branch,
Denver Public Library, Colorado.

Online Selling

Collection: Books or DVDs about eBay or Craig's List

Props: Pair of shoes, figurine, tennis racket

Signage: "Trash Into Cash"

Opera

Collection: Books, music, and movies of and about opera, language dictionaries, biographies of opera singers

Props: Brocade cloth

Signage: None

Optimism Month

> Collection: Self-help and positive-thinking titles
>
> Props: Glasses half full of blue paper to simulate water
>
> Signage: "March Is National Optimism Month"

National Optimism Month display. Schlessman Family Branch, Denver Public Library, Colorado.

Pamper Yourself

> Collection: Aromatherapy and home beauty titles
>
> Props: Candles, jars of flowers and bath salts
>
> Signage: "Pamper Yourself" or "Take Me Away"

Spa display. Schlessman Family Branch, Denver Public Library, Colorado.

Parties

Collection: Books about hosting, planning, and organizing parties

Props: Party hat

Signage: "Have a Ball" or "Let Me Entertain You"

Poetry

Collection: Poetry, biographies of poets, guides to writing and publishing poetry, poetry magazines

Props: Bucket of fake grass

Signage: "A Poet and Didn't Even Know It"

Politics

Collection: Biographies by and about politicians; political writings by politicians; political satires

Props: Red and blue fabric, toy elephant and donkey

Signage: "On the Campaign Trail"

Rock-and-Roll Fiction

Collection: Fiction about rock and roll

Props: LPs or a toy electric guitar

Signage: "Rock and Read"

Royalty

Collection: Fiction and nonfiction about royalty

Props: Purple velvet and tiara

Signage: "Regal Royals"

Sewing

Collection: Books and audiovisuals about fashion and sewing

Props: Fabric, spools of thread, tape measure, old patterns

Signage: "Threadbangers" or "Sew Much"

Slow Cooking

Collection: Slow cooking, crock pot cookery

Props: Crockpot filled with silk fall leaves

Signage: "Time for the Crock Pot"

Space

Collection: Books and audiovisuals about space

Props: Toy planets and space shuttle

Signage: "I'm Outer Here"

**National Astronomy Week display. Schlessman Family Branch,
Denver Public Library, Colorado.**

Titanic

Collection: Fiction and nonfiction about the *Titanic*

Props: Life preserver, best seller list from 1912

Signage: "Unsinkable"

Tear Jerkers

Collection: Sad or bittersweet fiction

Props: Tissue box

Signage: "Tear Jerkers" or "Need a Good Cry?"

Tear Jerkers. Saxton B. Little Free Library, Columbia, Connecticut.

Travel Survival

Collection: Travel etiquette, bargain guides, how to pack, easy phrase books

Props: Bottle of water

Signage: "Come Back Alive"

Traveling with Children

Collection: Travel guides specifically for children's activities, game books

Props: Suitcase filled with toys

Signage: "Are We There Yet?"

Travel with Children display. Schlessman Family Branch, Denver Public Library, Colorado.

True Crime

Collection: Nonfiction true crime

Props: Plastic bloody knife, black glove

Signage: "In the Parlor with a Candlestick"

Vegetarian

Collection: Vegetarian/vegan cookbooks and nutritional books

Props: Fake vegetables

Signage: "Eat Your Veggies"

You've Got Mail

Collection: Books that include or are about letters and correspondence

Props: Old letters, stamps, mailbox

Signage: "You've Got Mail"

GLOSSARY

CPS Collection presentation standards. Presentation techniques within the run of traditional shelving.

Display A stand-alone themed arrangement.

Facing Showing off the cover of the item.

The Floor Any public area in the library.

Fluffing Straightening, arranging, and putting a display back in order. Also can include restocking merchandise.

Fronting Pulling the item to the front of the shelf or display unit.

Key Areas Areas to emphasize with displays and merchandising. The retail world refers to this as zones.

Merchandiser Staff member responsible for displays, product placement, and quality and attractiveness of merchandise.

Merchandising A methodical, artistic use of space to promote a product.

Planogram Blueprint that details how a display is set up. Also called a schematic.

POCO Point of check out. The retail world refers to this as point of sale (POS) or point of purchase (POP).

Power Wall A wall that displays a dominant story or theme. Usually adjacent to the entrance.

Products Library collection.

Props Items use to convey or accentuate the display theme.

Traffic Flow The pattern that customers travel through the space.

Vignettes An arrangement of props, supporting material, and signage that instantly convey the theme of a display.

Index

About the Authors

JENNY LAPERRIERE is currently the Senior Librarian at the Schlessman Family Branch of the Denver Public Library. She has been the director of two small public libraries, Head of Technical Services for a medium public library, and Catalog Librarian for a State Library.

TRISH CHRISTIANSEN has worked for many different retail companies and has over ten years of retail merchandising experience. She has been with the Denver Public Library for five years.

Visit the authors' blog at www.librarymerchandising@blogspot.com.